How to Take Perfect
Scrapbook Pictures

by Joann Zocchi

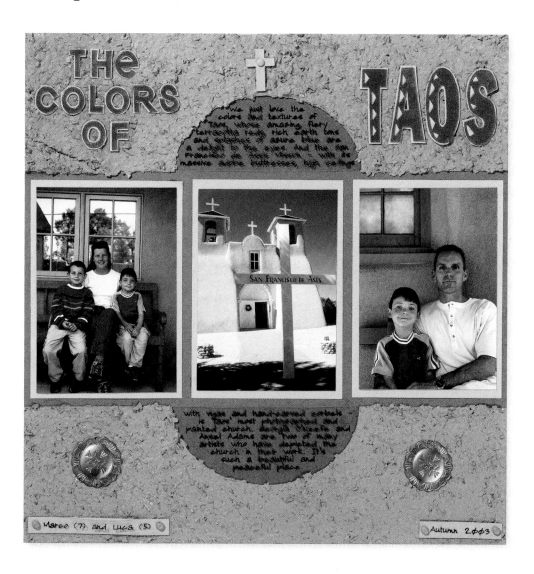

MEMORY MAKERS BOOKS

Memory Makers Books

Author and Photographer Joann Zocchi

Senior Editor MaryJo Regier

Art Director Nick Nyffeler

Graphic Designers Robin Rozum, Andrea Zocchi

Craft Editor Jodi Amidei

Art Acquisitions Editor Janetta Abucejo Wieneke

Photographer Ken Trujillo

Contributing Photographers Steve Brettler, Lizzy Creazzo, Susan Cyrus, Paula DeReamer, Angela Kelly, Brenda Martinez, Kelli Noto, Eric Paddock, Sandy Puc, Tory Read, Jennifer Reeves, MaryJo Regier, Stephen Tourlentes, Ken Trujillo, Andrea Zocchi, Joann Zocchi

Contributing Artists Jodi Amidei, Cori Dahmen, Paula DeReamer, Laurel Gervitz, Barb Hogan, Pamela James, Nicole LaCour, Bay Loftis, Shelley Rankin, MaryJo Regier, Becky Thompson, Shelby Valadez, Holly VanDyne, Cherie Ward, Leah Blanco Williams, MaryAnn Wise

Contributing Memory Makers Masters Joanna Bolick, Jennifer Bourgeault, Susan Cyrus, Shannon Taylor, Denise Tucker

Editorial Support Karen Cain, Emily Curry Hitchingham, Lydia Rueger, Dena Twinem

Memory Makers® How to Take Perfect Scrapbook Pictures

Published by Memory Makers Books, an imprint of F+W Publications, Inc.

12365 Huron Street, Suite 500, Denver, CO 80234

Phone 1-800-254-9124

First edition. Printed in the United States.

09 08 07 06 05   5 4 3 2 1

Library of Congress Cataloging-in-Publication Data

Zocchi, Joann, 1962-
    How to take perfect scrapbook pictures / by Joann Zocchi.
        p. cm.
    Includes bibliographical references and index.
    ISBN 1-892127-40-7
      1. Photography--Handbooks, manuals, etc. 2. Scrapbooks--Handbooks, manuals, etc. I.
Title.

TR146.Z625 2005
771--dc22   2004062588

Distributed to trade and art markets by

F+W Publications, Inc.

4700 East Galbraith Road, Cincinnati, OH 45236

Phone 1-800-289-0963

ISBN 1-892127-40-7

Memory Makers Books is the home of *Memory Makers*, the scrapbook magazine dedicated to educating and inspiring scrapbookers. To subscribe, or for more information, call 1-800-366-6465. Visit us on the Internet at www.memorymakersmagazine.com.

This book belongs to

_____

This book is dedicated to my husband, Andrea, who has helped me to become the photographer that I am today; and to my children, Marco and Luca, who have taught me to see the wonder in everything.

This book is also dedicated to the reader with great hopes that the beautiful images you strive to make will soon be in your hands. There is no greater feeling of accomplishment than making an image that truly captures the essence of the moment.

Special thanks to MaryJo Regier, Nick Nyffeler, Ken Trujillo and the staff at Memory Makers Books for guiding me through this project. Thank you also to Barbara Kotsos and Janette Reynolds of Epson America, Inc. for their expert advice and technical support.

Finally, I would like to thank Steve Brettler, Angela Kelly, Eric Paddock, Sandy Puc, Tory Read, Stephen Tourlentes and Ken Trujillo for their words of wisdom and terrific photographs.

Table of Contents

Working With Light 48-57

Visual Dynamics: Giving Your Photographs Impact 58-69

Photographing People 70-87

Every Picture Tells a Story 88-105

Watching your kids grow and become such individual souls is probably one of life's greatest joys. Each child bringing unique qualities that shine through in many different ways. Such treasures make each day an exciting adventure for a growing family. October 2004

Introduction

I have been photographing ever since I was 12. From the moment that I shot my first roll of film, I fell in love with photography. My passion to know everything about photography turned me from a mediocre student and somewhat of a trouble-maker into a serious artist. I attended the Massachusetts College of Art where I earned both a Bachelors and Masters of Fine Art degrees in photography. Today I am a professional artist, assistant professor at the University of Colorado at Denver and Health Sciences Center, and the mother of two beautiful boys. In my artwork I am inspired by the unique ability of photography to tell vivid stories that transport the viewer to exciting places. For the past fifteen years, my own photographic work has concentrated on environmental and conservation issues. I have had the privilege of showing my work all over the world, and I couldn't imagine a more rewarding profession.

My second love is teaching. I have the great joy of sharing what I know with others so that they, too, might realize their own creative vision. I believe that we never stop learning. In fact, after I had my two children, I started looking at my camera as a different kind of tool. As a mother, I keep my camera close by to capture those unique and important moments. I live with these photographs of my family and they are my most precious possessions.

In this book I combine my two loves, photography and teaching, and it is my sincere wish that you, the reader, will benefit. Whether you are a beginner or an advanced photographer, this book will teach you the technical and creative skills you need to make exciting photographs. You will learn how to take photographs that will capture those one-of-a-kind moments with dynamic visual impact. This book provides easy-to-understand explanations in plain English with inspiring illustrations to help you master the skills you need to make every photograph fantastic. I am excited for your journey into the heart of photography and trust that your quest to make every photograph a great one will be realized.

Joann

Joann Zocchi
Author & Photographer
How To Take Perfect Scrapbook Pictures

Camera Basics

There are many different types of cameras on the market today, from fully automatic point-and-shoot cameras to the latest digital SLRs. Every type of camera has unique qualities that affect the image and the range of creative possibilities that the photographer has to choose from.

If you already have a camera, this chapter will help you better understand how your camera works and its strengths. If you are in the market for a new camera, this chapter will give you the information that you need to purchase the camera that is right for you.

Wonderful photographs can be made with any type of camera, and the more you know about how to use your camera the better your photographs will be. A camera is a tool—like a sculptor's chisel or a painter's brush. It is the artist—in this case, the photographer—who makes something of beauty—but a good tool does help.

Jack and Luca were instant friends long before the tiki birthday party, but it became even stronger as they played together on this beautiful afternoon. Jack is a bit more reserved than Luca but they melded quickly and bonded together on all

Camera Basics

Everything in photography starts with the camera. The camera defines how the image will look and determines the way a photographer can shoot. Getting to know your camera is the single most significant thing that you can do to improve your images. With a little bit of time and practice, the rewards will be tremendous. The more you know about your camera, the better your photographs will be.

THE CAMERA A camera is a device that captures light reflecting off of an object and records that light onto light-sensitive media (film or, in the case of digital cameras, an electronic chip). Images can be made in a wide variety of lighting conditions by adjusting the amount of light that reaches the media. The amount of light reaching the media is controlled by two camera functions. The first is aperture. Located in the lens, the aperture is an adjustable opening or diaphragm that allows a measured amount of light into the camera.

TIP: When taking a light meter reading, avoid the brightest and the darkest areas. Seek an area with an equal balance of light and dark or a middle tone.

Larger aperture openings allow more light to reach the film while smaller aperture openings let in less light. The mechanism that controls the amount of time that the light exposes the film is called the shutter. The shutter is a curtain located in the camera body that opens and closes in measured increments of time allowing light to reach the film.

EXPOSURE Photographs look best with a full range of detail in the highlights and shadow areas and a smooth transition of tones across the middle range. The quality of the image depends upon the film or digital chip getting exposed to the right amount of light. Overexposure is caused by too much light reaching the film or chip and will result in images that print very light with little detail in the highlights. Underexposure will occur when not enough light has reached the film. The resulting print will be very dark with no detail in the shadows. Your camera is equipped with a light meter that measures the light in the scene and suggests an aperture opening and shutter speed combination that will produce the best exposure.

LIGHT-METER READINGS To create a terrific exposure, you begin by pointing your camera at your subject and engaging the light meter to take a reading. The light meter reads the light and indicates whether the current aperture and shutter speed settings are correct. If they are not correct, it will indicate that changes need to be made.

Proper exposure

Underexposed

Overexposed

Taos, New Mexico, is full of brilliant color. The first image is a perfect exposure that captures a wide range of tones and the brilliant colors that are characteristic of the region. The second image is underexposed, causing the image to be too dark with little detail in the shadow areas. The third image is overexposed, caused by too much light reaching the film or digital chip resulting in an image that is too light.

Skill builder

Find a scene that has a wide range of light areas and dark areas. Identify the bright area of the scene, take a light-meter reading in the bright area and photograph that area. Identify the dark area of the scene, take a light-meter reading in the dark area and photograph that area. Then identify an area of the scene that has an equal mix of light and dark areas and take the shot. When you get the images back, notice how the light in particular areas affects the light meter and the final exposure.

Operating Modes

All cameras are designed with at least one, and often a half dozen, operating modes. These different modes determine the exposure of the film or chip given various shooting situations.

MANUAL MODE In the manual mode a correct exposure is made when the photographer adjusts both the aperture (the opening in the lens) and shutter speed (the timed curtain) to balance the light meter.

APERTURE-PRIORITY MODE Aperture priority is a semiautomatic mode that allows the photographer to select the aperture while the camera selects the shutter speed.

SHUTTER-PRIORITY MODE Shutter priority is a semi-automatic mode that allows the photographer to set the shutter speed while the camera selects the aperture opening.

This image of the Grand Canyon shows how the landscape mode reproduces sharp focus throughout the space.

PROGRAM MODE Most modern cameras have a program-mode feature that is indicated with the letter "P" for programmed exposure. In the program mode, the camera will select both the correct shutter speed and aperture opening to achieve a balanced light-meter reading.

SUBJECT MODE Some cameras have programmed modes that are designed to work with specific shooting situations such as landscape, portraiture, close-up and action/sports. When a subject mode is selected, the camera automatically sets the optimum aperture opening and shutter-speed combination for the subject.

This photograph of a wind surfer shows how the action/sports mode can be used to stop movement. In the action/sports mode the camera automatically selects a fast shutter speed and the aperture opening needed to make a correct exposure.

Photographing in the subject mode is convenient and easy when you do not have time to think about the camera adjustments. In the portrait mode the camera selects an aperture opening that will create a shallow depth of field. With the background out of focus, the viewer's attention goes right to the individuals photographed.

Skill builder

Get to know what your operating modes are by shooting the same exact image in every mode that your camera is capable of. Set up a scene, recruit a friend or find a place where you can shoot an entire roll of film at one time. Take along paper and pen to take notes. Set the camera up to photograph the scene, and keep it in the exact same place for every shot. Adjust your camera to one of your operating modes and take the photograph. Write down the frame number, the mode you used and the camera's aperture and shutter-speed settings used to take the shot. Switch to the next operating mode, take the shot and make notes. Continue working like this through all of your operating modes. After your images are processed, evaluate the photographs to see how the modes you used affected the images.

Lenses

Often overlooked, the lens is one of the most important pieces of equipment you have in your camera bag because it determines how the image will look. The lens controls the amount of light reaching the film, the sharpness of the image, the size of the subject in the frame and the angle of view. Most professional photographers carry a number of lenses with them when they photograph.

NORMAL LENS
For 35mm cameras, a 50mm or 55mm lens is considered normal. A normal lens reproduces the scene without distortion and is closest to what the human eye sees. A normal lens is a good, all-purpose choice.

WIDE-ANGLE LENS
A wide-angle lens will reproduce a wider view capturing more of the scene than a normal lens and, depending on how wide the lens is, can distort the perspective in the image. The most common wide-angle lenses for 35mm cameras are 24mm, 28mm and 35mm. Extreme wide-angle lenses are sometimes referred to as "fish-eye" lenses. Wide-angle lenses are good for photographing interiors and large objects up close—like the facade of a church—and landscapes.

TELEPHOTO LENS
A telephoto lens will make the subject appear closer than it actually is. A telephoto lens produces a narrow angle of view, compresses the image by making objects in the scene appear closer together, and reproduces a more narrow range of focus than normal or wide-angle lenses. Common telephoto lenses for 35mm cameras include 80mm, 120mm and 200mm—which are super for creating dramatic portraits and capturing wildlife and sports-action photographs.

ZOOM LENS
A zoom lens is many lenses in one. A zoom lens can shift from a wide angle, through normal to a telephoto lens by simply turning a ring on the lens barrel or pressing a button on the camera body. Many photographers like the convenience and speed of carrying around one zoom lens that can do it all.

MACRO LENS
A macro lens is designed to photograph objects up close. A macro lens allows the photographer to create a close-up image such as a ladybug sitting on a blade of grass or a dew-covered spider web. Most non-macro lenses cannot focus so closely.

Skill builder

Shoot the same exact scene with every lens that you have. This will help you see exactly how each lens changes the image.

The sculpture museum in Florence is rich in color and full of incredible objects—a perfect place to explore how the lens you use can transform an image. This series of images were all created while standing in the same place. Three different lenses were used: a 28mm, 50mm and 85mm.

28mm lens (wide angle)

50mm lens (normal)

85mm lens (telephoto)

SLR Cameras

The most common camera used by professional photographers is the SLR or single lens reflex camera. Today's user-friendly SLRs can help you shoot like a pro! SLRs give the photographer the widest range of creative choices because of their versatility and exposure controls. SLRs have interchangeable lenses that greatly expand the visual possibilities. Taking advantage of all that SLRs have to offer takes time, patience and practice, but once the skills are learned, the sky is the limit.

AN SLR IS RIGHT FOR YOU IF:

• You want the most creative control possible
• You would like to use a variety of lenses
• You would like a camera that will grow with you
  as you build technical expertise
• You are willing to take the time to learn how to use it
• You are willing to carry a heavier camera and its accessories

Skill builder

Carry around a small notebook and make notes about the photographs you make. List the frame number, aperture setting, shutter-speed setting, any shooting mode you may have used, notes about the scene and information about the lighting conditions. When reviewing the final images made, have a look at your notes to see what you did for each shot. Identify what worked well and what didn't work well. Taking notes and evaluating your final images will help you become an expert at using your camera.

TIP: If you use an SLR camera, consider adding a compact point-and-shoot camera to your camera bag. Use the SLR as your primary camera and your point-and-shoot to capture those fleeting moments that are often lost by taking time to adjust and set your SLR. Shooting with both an SLR and compact point-and-shoot will increase your potential to capture all aspects of your experiences. It is especially handy to have both when photographing important events or traveling.

Long the workhorse of many professional photographers, SLR models come in all shapes and sizes. Some SLRs are strictly controlled manually by the photographer while others have fully automatic features with manual-override capabilities. SLR cameras provide the widest range of creative control for the photographer because of their versatility and wide array of lenses and accessories.

Digital Cameras

Digital cameras are becoming more and more popular with photographers today. Rather than using film technology to capture the image, digital cameras use an image-sensor chip that captures the image in pixels and then stores the image in memory. Most digital cameras have built-in LCD screens that allow you to review and edit your photographs instantly. After shooting or capturing an image, the digital image file can be downloaded from the camera's memory directly into a computer or printed on a digital printer. Photographers interested in using a digital camera can choose from compact point-and-shoots to professional quality SLR cameras with interchangeable lenses.

RESOLUTION Resolution refers to the amount of detail captured in a digital image. The higher the resolution, the finer the image will be. Every digital image is made up of tiny photograph elements called pixels. The resolution of the image identifies the exact number of pixels present. Camera costs and image quality are in direct relationship to the resolution that the camera can capture. Resolution not only affects image quality but enlargement potential. A 3-megapixel image will hold good, photographic-quality detail when printed no larger than 8 x 10". A 5-megapixel image will hold good, photographic-quality detail when printed no larger than 11 x 14".

A DIGITAL CAMERA IS RIGHT FOR YOU IF:

• You would like to edit your images as you take them

• You would like the option of manipulating and retouching your own images

• You would like to print your own images

• You are willing to take the time to learn the technology

• You are willing to pay more up front and save on film costs down the road

• Remember! If you want good, quality images, you have to pay for a higher resolution camera.

Digital cameras come in all shapes and sizes with varying degrees of resolution capabilities and accessories with which to experiment. Some digital cameras will come with their own software and/or downloading cable or "dock." Most all digital cameras provide you with an option for increasing memory through the use of memory cards, some of which you can insert directly into certain printers as opposed to downloading the images to your computer before you can print.

TIP: Make a mini tool kit for your camera bag. Include a small Swiss army knife with a screwdriver, a miniature roll of duct tape and a bit of jeweler's wire. These items can help you fix camera-bag contents in a pinch.

Compact Point-and-Shoot Cameras

Point-and-shoot cameras are convenient and extremely easy to use. Many are equipped with fully automatic features that allow the photographer to capture images without having to worry about camera functions. Their compact size makes them very portable and most can fit in a shirt pocket. Compact cameras come in a staggering range of models and features. Most are relatively inexpensive, but a caveat: A camera is only as good as the lens. Even the most advanced features cannot compensate for a lens that does not take sharp, clear photographs.

A POINT-AND-SHOOT IS RIGHT FOR YOU IF:
• You want something small to fit in a pocket or purse
• You simply want to take photographs without thinking about camera functions
• You will be using your camera in hostile environments, such as the beach or boating, and don't want to ruin an expensive digital or SLR camera
• You need to travel light
• You know that if a camera is too big you will never take it with you

Single-Use Cameras

Single-use (or disposable) cameras are immense fun to shoot with. These plastic cameras come with film already loaded and ready to go. Many single-use cameras come with a flash feature that allows you to photograph in a variety of lighting situations. The most important factor when choosing which camera to use is the lighting condition you will be photographing in. Single-use cameras come with a specific ISO (speed) film loaded into the camera. If you are shooting in low-light situations, purchase a camera loaded with 400 ISO film or faster. In bright-light situations, use a camera that has a lower ISO rating of 200 ISO or lower. Some manufacturers also make waterproof single-use cameras that can be submerged.

TIP: Give your kids their own single-use cameras and see the world from their point of view. For events such as weddings, anniversaries and family reunions, hand out single-use cameras to the guests and make them the photographers. Shoot with a single-use camera at the beach, boating, camping or in any situation where you don't feel comfortable bringing an expensive camera that could be damaged.

Compact point-and-shoot cameras are similar in size to the many single-use cameras available on the market and all make for quick-and-easy shooting in a pinch or on-the-go. Choosing the proper film speed in these cameras for shooting indoors or out will provide the best results.

Camera Accessories

No outfit is complete without the perfect accessories. Accessories allow you to expand your photographic possibilities. The right accessory can be the difference between a good photograph and no photograph at all.

FLASH If your camera does not already have one, a flash is a must-have addition to your equipment. A flash will allow you to photograph in low-light situations and at night. A flash can be used in combination with sunlight to lighten harsh shadows and give a professional look to your images.

TRIPOD AND CABLE RELEASE A tripod and cable release allow you to stabilize your camera for slow exposures. During slow exposures the tripod will keep your camera from shaking which results in blurred images. The cable release attaches to the shutter-release button and helps to prevent the shaking that can occur when you take the photograph. Many new cameras come with a remote-control feature that allows you to trip the shutter remotely. This is an excellent alternative to the unpredictable self-timer feature on most cameras.

FILTERS Filters modify the way an image looks. Colored filters can be used to enhance or alter the original color of the subject photographed. A polarizing filter reduces, and can even eliminate, unwanted glare from reflective objects in the scene. A graduated neutral-density filter can increase the detail in the sky adding drama to any landscape. A starburst filter will turn reflections on water into a blanket of diamonds and a soft-focus filter will create a glowing effect around the highlights of your subject. When purchasing a filter for your camera, be sure to match the size of the filter with the circumference of your lens or lenses.

CAMERA BAGS Camera bags come in a wide variety of colors, shapes, styles and sizes all designed to store and protect your camera equipment. Look for a well-padded bag that holds all of your equipment comfortably. Choose a bag that you will be comfortable holding for long periods of time. Camera bags that allow you to rearrange the padded compartments on the inside are the most versatile because they can be changed to suit your needs.

TIP: Don't forget batteries. There is nothing worse than having to stop photographing because your battery is spent and you do not have extra batteries in your camera bag. Always carry extra batteries. Refer to your camera or camera manual to find out exactly what kind of batteries your camera takes and don't forget to stock up on extra batteries for your flash.

Using a graduated warming filter transformed this scene into graphic bands of color that accentuate the orange glow of the setting sun.

A starburst filter turns ordinary reflections into extraordinary light that truly captures the magic of the Grand Canal in Venice, Italy.

A soft-focus filter changes both the look and feel of images, turning this portrait into a touching and beautiful moment. Photo: Ellen Hargrove, Jenks, Oklahoma

Expert Advice: What Camera Is Right for You?

Steve Brettler, Owner, E.P. Levine

PURCHASING A CAMERA

Purchasing a camera can be a daunting task to be sure. Today you can choose between hundreds of different types, models and price ranges. There is a good deal to determine before you decide to part with your hard-earned cash.

CONSIDER A CAMERA'S FEATURES

Most cameras have become generalists, particularly in this age of computer-chip driven products. It seems so easy to add features to cameras, it frequently appears that most cameras have too many. But even so, each camera implements features in a different way and this can skew the usability toward a different type of use. If you can identify in advance what specialized features that you want in a camera, you will be able to rule out a lot of choices.

FINDING A GOOD BUY

Didn't your mother tell you that you get what you pay for? Mine did and she also told me that a deal that's too good to be true most often is. Both rules hold true when camera shopping. But don't get duped into spending more than you want either. Shop around and become an informed consumer, but keep in mind that the best value is not always the lowest price.

Here you have almost as many choices as you do with cameras. The Internet, national discount chains, local specialty stores and your uncle Fred are all viable options, but each has its own trade-offs that balance price and service. And while the Internet represents the ultimate in terms of convenience and the ability to compare prices, it may not be the best place for everyone to shop. Oftentimes specialty camera stores have nearly as competitive of prices and can provide a wealth of knowledge and support for the novice or first-time purchaser. And even if the price is a bit higher than what your local discounter or Internet merchant charges, perhaps it's worth it. You now have a relationship you can count on to provide service and support throughout your photograph-making career.

No matter where you make your purchase, check to be sure you are getting a legitimate U.S. importer's warranty. Most camera stores that specialize in used equipment will offer you not only a warranty of some sort but also the ability to exchange all or part of your purchase within a reasonable amount of time just in case you change your mind.

STEVE BRETTLER has been involved in photography in some form or another since his high school days and has been the owner and president of E.P. Levine since 1988. E.P. Levine is New England's premier equipment resource for professional photographers. Their specialty is personal service, knowledgeable sales staff and a huge inventory of both new and used photo gear, photographic supplies and consumables as well as products for digital imaging. In his spare time Steve is learning how to play the Uilleann (Irish) bagpipes. For more information about E.P. Levine, see Steve's Web site at www.cameras.com.

Film & Digital Media

Film and pixels are the "canvases of light" in photography. These light-sensitive materials capture and record the subtle nuances of light and transform them into images that inspire our imaginations. These fundamental elements of photography play a crucial role in the technical quality and visual characteristics of your photographic images.

Choosing the right film for the lighting conditions is one of the first creative decisions that a photographer must make. Knowing the differences between films and understanding how film is designed to work with light will greatly improve your images.

For those of you working in the digital realm, knowing how digital cameras read and translate light into images will strengthen your technical skills and the creative impact of your photographs. Understanding the canvas of light and knowing how to use it will inspire your creative eye to fully capture the rainbow of possibilities.

Color can be used to establish the mood of an image. The pastel color of the setting sun, mirrored in the surface of the water, creates a photograph that feels like a turn-of-the-century landscape painting.

The smooth and subtle tones of this black-and-white image capture the quiet peacefulness of sunrise and the morning fog lifting from the lake. In color, this image would not have had the same contemplative feel.

Film

Choices, choices, choices…what is the right film for you? Film defines many of the most important characteristics of an image. From black-and-white to color, the film you choose to use will significantly impact the way your images look. Film determines the amount of fine details captured, the color of the light recorded, the shutter speeds and aperture settings you can use, the number of images you will take and how large you can print a final image.

SENSITIVITY TO LIGHT Film manufacturers have created a wide variety of films designed to accommodate many different lighting situations. Some films are made to be very sensitive to light and are used in low-lighting situations. Other films are created with less sensitivity to light, designed for use in the bright light of a normal sunny day. How sensitive the film is to light can be identified by a system of numbers called the ISO. Films with an ISO rating of 400, 800, 1600 and 3200 are considered "fast" films. Films with an ISO rating of 100, 160 and 200 are considered intermediate, and films with an ISO rating of 64, 50 and 25 are "slow" films. Fast films are designed for low-light situations while slow films are designed for use in bright light.

IMAGE QUALITY Fine image detail is determined by the speed or ISO of the film. Slow-speed films have a lot of fine detail and fast-speed films have less. What you lose in lower image quality will be gained in your ability to shoot with faster shutter speeds and to record information in low-lighting situations. Because slower-speed films capture more information, they should be used if you are planning on making enlargements bigger than 11 x 14" because they will hold crisp details when printed big.

BLACK-AND-WHITE OR COLOR Photographers can purchase black-and-white or color films for their cameras. Choosing which one to use is a purely aesthetic choice made by the photographer. The issues of light sensitivity and image quality described above are the same for both kinds of film.

SLIDE FILM/TRANSPARENCIES Slide film, also referred to as transparency film, is the best film for recording brilliant, intense color and maximum detail. Slide films are easily identified by the use of the word "chrome" in the ending of the film name, such as Ektachrome and Fujichrome. However, transparency film is unforgiving and it is important to have very accurate exposures. With transparency film the final product is a slide; if you want prints, you will have the added step and cost of making prints or scans.

Print Film/Negative Film

Print film produces a negative, in black-and-white or color, which can be printed on photographic paper or scanned into a computer. Color negative film is the choice of most amateur photographers today because of quick processing options and universal availability. If you are using color-print film, choose an ISO or film speed and brand that works and looks best to you. Different manufacturers' films each have various color biases; try a few different kinds to determine which film you like best. To choose the right film for the lighting conditions, try this:

EXPOSURES Film manufacturers produce film with three different choices in the number of exposures per roll. A 12-exposure roll is a great choice if you know that you only want to shoot a small number of images or if you want to change to another kind of film fairly quickly. Film rolls with 24 exposures are very popular because they have just the right number of exposures that you might need to shoot one event. Film rolls with 36 exposures are handy when you know that you will be shooting a lot of images and do not want to stop to change film right in the middle of all the action.

To capture the intricate detail of this church dome in Italy requires some thoughtful consideration about film. A fast-speed film would make photographing this scene easy to do without a tripod but the subtle color and details would be lost in the grain of the film. In this low-light situation, a slower-speed film requires the use of a tripod but is well worth the extra effort because slower-speed film reveals the fine craftsmanship of the dome.

Bright and contrasty light—such as the light surrounding this church in Taos, New Mexico—creates a challenge to capture a full range of details in both the highlights and the shadow areas. In these kinds of lighting situations, slide film is a perfect choice because it can record a broader range of tones than color-negative film.

One Determine if you want to photograph the event in black-and-white or color.

Two Determine if you want to shoot slide film or negative film.

Three Evaluate the lighting situation and pick the film that is designed for that lighting situation. If you will be shooting in the evening, choose a faster-speed film such as ISO 400. If you will be outside all day on a sunny picnic, shoot an intermediate-speed film such as ISO 100. If you need to shoot in a variety of lighting conditions with only one roll of film, try ISO 200 and bring your flash.

Four Determine how many images you might shoot and choose the number of exposures that will accommodate the situation.

Skill builder

Build your knowledge of film by creating your own film test. Purchase three rolls of film that have a variety of speeds such as 100, 400 and 1600. Shoot all three rolls of film in a variety of lighting conditions. The test will be even more effective if you shoot the same exact subjects in the same lighting conditions for each roll. After the images are processed, evaluate how each film handled the lighting conditions and subject matter that you shot.

The Color of Light

Capturing light accurately is a balancing act that requires the photographer to know how film records the color of light. Have you ever noticed the cool green color of a fluorescent light fixture or the yellow-orange glow surrounding your table lamp? Light sources such as the sun, a tungsten bulb and a fluorescent tube emit very specific wavelengths of color, but our sophisticated vision corrects for these color shifts and presents us with images that appear to have "normal" realistic color.

DAYLIGHT Color film records the color of the light that it sees without interpretation. To correct shifts in color and reproduce realistic color on film, manufacturers have designed two main types of color film. Daylight-balanced film is the most commonly used color film that will produce accurate color when shot with sunlight or a flash as the light source. If daylight film is shot under tungsten light, the image will have a reddish-orange color that is very difficult to remove completely when printing. If daylight film is shot under fluorescent lights, the image will have a greenish colorcast.

TUNGSTEN LIGHT Tungsten film is designed to produce accurate color under tungsten light sources such as a common household light bulb. Used primarily by professional photographers, it is ideal for photographing interiors lit by tungsten light or when copying artwork under tungsten lights. Shooting tungsten-balanced film in daylight will produce images that have a blue cast and should be avoided.

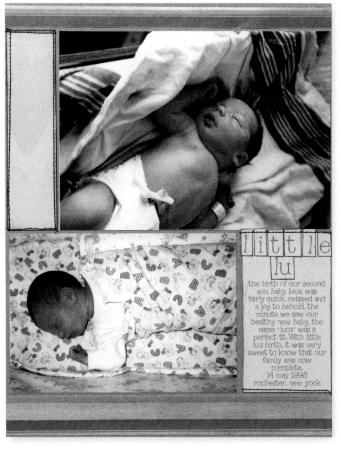

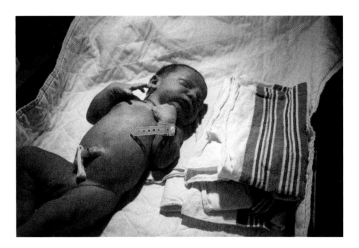

Daylight film shot under tungsten light creates a yellow-orange cast but there are times when using a flash to color correct the image is simply not possible. This photograph of my newborn son benefits from the orange glow as it creates a warm and sentimental quality to the moment.

The green glow of fluorescent lights on daylight film transforms this image by giving it an ethereal feel and unusual look.

Balancing Light

Film is designed to reproduce natural color under very specific lighting situations such as daylight or tungsten light. If you are like most photographers who shoot one roll of film in a variety of places, you will no doubt encounter lighting situations that are not the right mix for the film that you are shooting. With the help of your flash and a little imagination you can make the most of every lighting situation you encounter.

USING A FLASH TO CORRECT A COLOR IMBALANCE
If you are shooting with daylight film in a space that has another kind of light source, such as sodium vapor, fluorescent or tungsten lights, you can reduce unwanted color by using your flash. The output of the flash has the same color temperature or color balance as daylight and will fill the area with the color of light that the film is designed to reproduce accurately.

MIXING LIGHT SOURCES FOR TERRIFIC COLOR IMAGES
Once you have learned how to get rid of unwanted color shifts, I encourage you to use color shifts to create surprising and unexpected color images. Many distinguished photographers shooting color film mix a variety of light sources together. The results are dynamic color combinations that delight the eyes. A good place to start is to combine natural and artificial light together with both tungsten and daylight-balanced film. A good time of day to find these kinds of combinations is in the early morning or late afternoon when the streetlights are lit and the sun is on the edge of the horizon. Try mixing a tungsten light source with the daylight streaming in from an open window. Combining natural and artificial light sources in the same image will bring together cool and warm colors, the ideal color combination for dramatic visual effect.

TIP: For more pleasing skin tones in your portrait photographs, buy a slight warming filter, such as an 81A. The filter will add an attractive warm hue to skin tone, eliminating some of the green and blue colors that often appear.

These images, from the cellar of an ancient villa in Italy, were shot using daylight film. The scene was illuminated with one sodium-vapor light and a small window off to the left. When photographed without the use of a flash, the sodium-vapor light recorded as deep orange on film. In this situation a flash was used to color correct the image. Because the flash output is more intense than the light coming from the sodium-vapor fixture, the flash neutralizes the color and has the additional effect of creating more light for a better exposure.

Superb processing really does make a difference. The range of tones captured in this image requires terrific processing to re-create the full range of tones in the original scene.

Buying & Processing Film

As photographers, we strive to capture once-in-a-lifetime moments that describe the beauty of our lives. Through photography, we celebrate the birth of babies, graduations, birthday parties, weddings and anniversaries. Our photographs are passed down to the next generation so that our children can remember and dream. Creating lasting images that can withstand the test of time begins with the quality of the film we buy and careful, professional processing.

BUYING FILM Beyond ISO, number of exposures, and color balance, there are a few more things to consider as you learn about film choices. In stores today you will find professional, amateur and private-label films. Films designated as professional films will be found in the refrigerator of your professional photography supply store. Professional films are carefully manufactured, transported and stored. Professional films can be relied upon for their consistent image quality and exposure predictability. They are more expensive than amateur films but many professional photographers would not use anything else.

Some stores and mail-order houses sell a house brand or private-label film. These films usually come in a limited range of ISOs and are generally less expensive than major brands. You may find these films to your liking but a thorough test is always recommended. Some retailers also sell film that is past its expiration date. Cheap, expired film is always a bad bet. Check the expiration date on all the film you purchase. Get to know your professional camera store so that you can be sure that the film you buy is fresh and well cared for. Most professional film retailers will give a discount for larger quantities sold at one time, usually 20-plus rolls.

TIP: To find a superb lab, start with recommendations then do a film-processing test. Drop off a roll of film to several different labs in your area. If the rolls are shot in similar lighting conditions, your test will be even more effective. Evaluate the quality of processing by comparing all rolls together.

Film that is not fresh or properly stored degrades quickly, losing the ability to reproduce a full range of tones and accurate color. Capturing details and subtle color of challenging lighting situations, like this photograph of a historic church in Italy, would not be possible with compromised film.

PROCESSING FILM Film processing, also referred to as developing, is another important factor in ensuring the quality of your final images. When your film is properly processed, you can count on the images to look their best even when printed very large. To make the best choices about film processing, it helps to understand that different types of film require different types of chemical processes for development. Black-and-white film can be processed in a wide range of chemical developers that artists and professionals choose based on the way they want the film to look. At photographic labs black-and-white films are generally processed in large, automated machines and in standard film developers. Some labs offer custom processing that is more expensive but allows specific results to be achieved.

Color-negative film is processed in C-41 chemistry by automated machines. Color slide films are also processed in automated machines. Ektachrome films are processed in E-6 chemistry and Kodachrome film is processed in K-14 chemicals. Sometimes photographers refer to their film in terms of the developing processing, such as E-6 for color slide or C-41 for color-negative film.

Choosing the lab that processes your film is important. Professional labs cater to professional photographers who risk losing thousands of dollars if the film is mishandled or ruined in the processing. Professional labs tend to be more expensive, but knowledgeable and attentive sales people will be able to help you with any questions you might have. Amateur labs, like film-processing chains and groceries stores, either process the film in their own mini labs or send it to larger, central facilities to be processed. Amateur labs that do a good job monitoring their chemistry and keeping their equipment clean can give excellent results. Choose a lab that gives you the best service, consistent processing results and clean negatives that are never damaged. Ask friends about labs they use or do a processing test. Many labs now offer digital scans on a CD with your processing if this service is requested.

Digital Media

Working in the digital realm requires photographers to anticipate how they are going to use the images that they make. Photographers who work digitally can design their images to be printed, e-mailed or loaded onto a Web site. To create the best possible end result, photographers need to make choices even before they start photographing. Understanding digital media is the first step toward making digital images that look remarkable in whatever way they are used.

PIXELS VS. FILM
Pixels are the light-sensitive bits of information in a digital image. Each pixel is a tiny square receptor that records the light falling onto it. Pixels can be compared to the tiny dots of photographic information on film called grain. Film-based images can contain millions of tiny dots of information that can produce minute detail and give the illusion of exact sharpness. In digital photography the number of pixels contained in an image is in direct relationship to the quality of the image. Digital images can contain millions of pixels and the greater the number of pixels, the finer the image will be. The exact number of pixels present in an image is referred to as the resolution.

IMAGE FORMATS
After the digital image is captured in the camera, the image is stored and saved in the camera's memory. Digital cameras have a variety of format options for saving images. Images can be saved as JPEG, TIFF or RAW file formats. The JPEG format is used to compress images, making them easier to send over the Internet. The greater amount of compression in a JPEG image, the lower the quality. The TIFF format is designed to prepare images for publishing and printing. TIFF images are also compressed but with no loss of information during the compression process. The RAW file format captures the image data as it has been recorded in the camera. RAW files are compressed but can be recompressed without any loss of information. RAW images are the highest quality and use up the most amount of space on the camera's memory as they are the largest in size.

IMAGE QUALITY
You can determine the quality and size of the image that the camera will capture. Compression and resolution affect the quality and size of your images. The amount of compression applied to an image is variable and chosen and set by the photographer. Remember that highly compressed images will lose quality but will take up less space in memory. Compression degrees are sometimes referred to as superfine, which is the least amount of compression; fine, which applies an intermediate amount of compression; and normal, which applies the most amount of compression. The resolution of every image can be adjusted from high resolution to low resolution and stops in between. High-resolution images contain the most pixels and low-resolution images contain the least amount of pixels.

The resolution of digital images affects the quality of the image. For printing purposes most digital images are created with a resolution of 300dpi. Images that are designed for use on Web sites are created with a resolution of 72dpi. These two images show how an image with a resolution of 72dpi will print compared to an image with a resolution of 300dpi. At 72dpi the image simply does not have enough digital information in the image to reproduce with a smooth transition of tones and the kind of detail that we would expect from a terrific image.

TRANSFERRING IMAGES FROM CAMERA
There are many ways to transfer images out of your camera and into a printer or your own computer. Many cameras connect directly to your digital printer through a connecting cable. You can send images directly from your camera to the printer. Or, you can bring the memory card to a participating photography lab for images to be printed out on their printers. With a connecting cable your camera can be connected to your computer and the images downloaded directly into your computer. Another way to get images into the computer is a memory-card reader that attaches to your computer and accepts the removable memory card from your camera and downloads the images onto your computer.

FILE SIZE
Digital images usually contain a large amount of information. High-resolution images with little compression take up a large amount of space and therefore have the greatest file size. To decrease file size you can either resize an image to make it smaller or use a file format that compresses the image such as JPEG. There are some software programs available that help you increase file size, but this usually results in poor-quality images. The good rule of thumb for digital images is never increase a file more than 120 percent.

Storage

It is easy to overlook how important it is to properly store your digital images, film and prints. Everything about photography culminates in the final print or digital file that we make. But you can't stop there. If you want your images to continue looking first-rate long into the future, you will need to know how to keep them safe.

DIGITAL STORAGE Images stored in your camera's memory or on your computer take up large quantities of valuable space that can be used for other things such as capturing new images or image editing. Some photographers add an additional hard drive onto their computers as a place designated to store digital images. Another solution that is becoming more affordable every day is to add a CD or DVD drive with read and write capabilities.

Recordable compact discs are the most commonly used storage devices on the market today. There are compact discs designed for recording images called CD-Rs that can only be recorded onto once. There are compact discs called CD-RW that are designed to be recorded onto multiple times when used in a CD-RW drive. CDs can store up to 700 megabytes of information and are easy to transport and store because they are small and thin. CD drives may be specifically designed to work with CD-Rs, CD-RWs, DVDs or all three. DVDs are another storage option that is slightly more expensive. Not every DVD can be read on a computer; you have to have a DVD drive to read a DVD. Holding up to 4.7 gigabytes of information, they are ideal for storing large numbers of images.

FILM STORAGE You will ruin your film by sticking it in the hot glove compartment of your car. The extreme heat will alter your film to the point of being unusable. Film should be stored in the original packaging and kept in a cool, dry place. You should always shoot your film before the expiration date that is printed on the outside of the package. It is also best to process your film as soon as you finish shooting it.

NEGATIVE, SLIDE AND PRINT STORAGE Storing your film and prints carefully is extremely important and often overlooked. If you want to make sure that your photographic treasures will be kept safe for the future, you must store them properly. Acid and polyvinyl chloride are the enemies of photographic media because they will eat away at your images over time. Archival storage requires acid- and PVC-free sleeves that will protect your images from breaking down. Fluctuating extremes in temperature will also degrade your originals, so store your sleeved negatives, slides and prints in acid-free boxes and PVC-free sleeves then store the boxes in a cool, dry and dark place.

TIP: As technology can sometimes fail, it is essential to have a number of copies of your digital files just in case. I always make two copies of my digital images. CDs and DVDs are not indestructible and will degrade over time. They should always be stored in a cool, dry place away from light and heat.

TIP: Oil and dirt from your hands can ruin a negative or a print with fingerprints and acid that will eat away your images over time. When handling negatives, transparencies and prints, make sure your hands are clean. If you want to keep your images in great shape for your children and their children, purchase a pair of acid-free cotton gloves at your local camera store. These gloves will ensure that your images will stay clean.

There are many retail stores that specialize in archival storage of film and prints. The key to longevity is to purchase storage supplies that are acid- and PVC-free.

Expert Advice: Preserving Film & Digital Media
Eric Paddock, Curator of Photography, Colorado Historical Society

CARE AND HANDLING

Tens of millions of photographs have been created since the medium was invented 170 years ago, yet only a fraction of them have survived. While some of those that disappeared were destroyed on purpose, most fell victim to the same preservation problems that we face today: rough handling, poor storage or display and the inherent vices of photographic media. No photograph will last forever, but with care and advanced planning, we can prolong the lives of our photographs so that others may enjoy them for many years to come.

For the longest photograph life, it is best to choose media that are known to last a long time and to use them correctly. Recent tests on improved color-photo papers indicate that they may hold their true colors for up to 75 years. Black-and-white negatives appear to be more stable than color films provided that they are correctly fixed and washed during the developing process. Digital photography poses new challenges in photography preservation because it involves new materials that we know comparatively little about. Accelerated aging tests indicate that some black-and-white digital prints will last as long as 200 years and that it is possible to make a digital color print that will not fade for 100 years. Unless we carefully match specific ink sets with particular papers, however, the results are likely to last for only a tenth of that time.

STORAGE

Storage looks complicated because so many products are available that it is hard to know or to choose what is best. Here's a clue: Even the best archival storage materials are worthless if they sit unused on a closet shelf, so pick the ones that you have time for. Choose acid-free, neutral-pH paper, mats and boxes.

If you care enough about your photographs to bother trying to preserve them, chances are that you like to look at them once in awhile too. A filing system that helps you find your photographs quickly and easily makes that possible and protects the photographs from wear and tear at the same time. I have seen collections that are filed by subject, date, project, theme, size and negative number. Those that are arranged by negative number work most efficiently because the same number can be used on the negative and any print that you make from it and you can create cross-reference lists using the numbers. Think about incorporating the date of the photo into the number. For example, the number 04.09.17.2.29 would identify the twenty-ninth photograph on the second roll of film taken on the 17th of September, 2004. Whichever care, handling and storage methods you use, proper techniques will add to the longevity of your images and make for easier access to them.

Gypsum, Colorado. Chromogenic Print. 2000 © Eric Paddock. All rights reserved.

ERIC PADDOCK is curator of photography at the Colorado Historical Society, where he works with a collection of 800,000 photographs—including everything from daguerreotypes to contemporary work—about Colorado and the American West. Eric is also an established and acclaimed photographic artist. His monograph book, *Belonging to the West*, was published in 1996, and his photographs are held in the collections of the Amon Carter Museum, the Bibliotheque Nationale, the Denver Art Museum, the Museum of Modern Art and the San Francisco Museum of Modern Art.

Pixel Perfect:
Understanding the Digital Domain

For more than a decade photographers have been hearing the rapidly approaching footsteps of digital photography. At first most photographers, I among them, were doubtful. Digital images were of poor quality, the computer power it took to process them was enormous and out of reach for most and the better digital cameras cost a small fortune. Today all that has changed; image quality improves with each new model year, computers are ultra fast with lots of memory and a good digital camera can be purchased for a reasonable price. What has also made this digital revolution possible is the abundance of good, inexpensive "photo quality" color printers.

Now you can make digital images that rival photographic prints at home. Digital photography adds another dimension to the photographic process with the ability to edit and manipulate the images you create. Image-editing software makes it possible to "improve" your images and add layers of creativity through photo collage, artistic effects and other types of manipulation previously unavailable.

The digital domain is changing all the time, and good photographic skills will allow you to take advantage of all the benefits that digital imaging has to offer. Remember the old computer adage "garbage in, garbage out." In other words good composition, exposure and understanding of your subject matter is crucial to any imaging process be it on film or recorded electronically on a computer chip.

Colors

I often remind myself to look at things as if it is through the lens of my camera. That is when I notice the colors of life, the details that surround us. The colors that bring such joy to the world and vivid life to the ordinary things we often forget to ponder. Such colors and details become so evident in photos, but it is also important to remind myself to find these things even when looking through my naked eyes and not focusing on anything but the beauty before me.

Hardware

Computers, printers and scanners are the basic hardware devices that photographers use to create images in their digital darkrooms. These pieces of equipment can determine the quality and size of the digital images that are produced. Designing or purchasing a digital darkroom that is right for you will require you to consider your budget as well as your needs.

COMPUTERS What is the best computer for digital imaging? This question, like many in the digital domain, has one definitive answer: It depends. It depends on the software programs that run on your computer. It depends on the way you intend to use your computer, whether for intensive image manipulation or just for sizing and minor image corrections. Most important, it depends on your budget.

WHAT BRAND DO I BUY? Most consumer computers fall into two categories. The first category is Apple MacIntosh computers, which run on Apple's own unique operating system. An OS, or operating system, is the software that makes the computer function. Think of the operating system as the basic language that your computer speaks. The second category, and by far the largest, is cumulatively referred to as PCs or personal computers. PCs run on Microsoft's Windows operating system. Which is the best? The answer to this question is "it depends." It depends on your needs and the software you want to use. It depends on whether you are already comfortable with one operating system or the other. And perhaps most important, if you are a novice, it depends on what operating system your spouse, kids or best friends are using. In the world of computers a knowledgeable friend is your most valuable resource.

WHAT FEATURES SHOULD MY COMPUTER HAVE? If the principle use of your computer is digital imaging, the most important feature is memory. Buy a computer with a large hard drive, the mechanism that stores data, and load it up with as much RAM (random access memory) as you can afford. Second on the list is processor speed. Usually measured in megahertz (MHz), the faster the processor, the quicker it will execute your commands. If your budget forces you to make a choice, go with a slightly slower computer processor but with more RAM. Other features that are valuable are a CD and/or DVD recorder and a large monitor. For working with images and image-manipulation programs, the minimum monitor size I would recommend would be 17". When buying a monitor, compare the resolution data, measured in "dot pitch," and the "refresh rate"; monitors with a refresh rate of less than 70MHz may cause eye fatigue.

The key pieces of hardware that many photographers use in their digital darkroom include a computer and monitor, flatbed/film scanner and a printer.

PRINTERS When choosing a printer ask yourself these questions: What is the largest print I intend to make? How many prints will I make in a printing session? Am I willing to pay more for better image quality, measured in dpi (dots per inch) and more fade-resistant inks? When you have answered these questions you will have a pretty good idea of what to look for in a printer. Don't forget to also price the actual ink and paper as that is where most of your cost will be over time. And always ask to see sample prints, preferably on the kind of paper you intend to use.

SCANNERS Scanners are input devices that allow computers to digitize flat artwork and photographs. Though not essential if you have a digital camera, they come in very handy and their cost is minimal. The most important attribute of a scanner is the "resolution" at which it is capable of rendering an image. The higher the resolution, the more detail in the digital image. If you don't have a digital camera, or you have lots of negatives and slides you would like to "digitize," make sure you buy a scanner that will allow you to scan slides and negatives. In this case it is even more important that your scanner have a minimum optical resolution of 1200dpi or higher.

Image-Editing Software

Software is a program that enables your computer to perform specific functions. We have already discussed the operating system that does basic things such as turning your computer on and off. Here we will discuss image-editing software designed to modify or manipulate images from your digital camera or those scanned into your computer.

There are many different image-editing software programs available. Most digital cameras include their own image-editing software and these software programs may meet your basic needs. However, if you intend to perform more advanced digital image manipulation, you will want a more powerful software package. Below is a list of basic and advanced features. These are general features and not found in all software packages; some may include more or fewer features.

BASIC FEATURES

- Acquires digital files in several digital formats such as JPEG and TIFF
- Adjusts the size and resolution of images
- Basic image adjustments/correction such as lightness/darkness, contrast and some color correction

ADVANCED FEATURES

- Includes all of the features above as well as the features listed below
- Has a sharpness/blur control for making the image more or less in focus
- Ability to combine multiple images to create photo collages and photomontages
- Clones or has the ability to copy an area of an image and apply it to another area
- Includes digital effects such as pastel, swirl and watercolor filters to name only a few
- Has multiple levels of undo, or "history," so if you are not pleased with the adjustments you have made you can return to your start point
- Has the ability to create sequences of commands that can be repeated with one click (very useful when processing many images)
- Includes many other advanced features too specific to explore here

This digital image of a colorful wagon wheel has terrific graphic qualities accentuated further by the saturation of the image. The saturation was increased to heighten the sense of color for greater visual impact.

The lists above give you a general idea. When researching image-editing software there is one current "gold standard" to be aware of: Adobe Photoshop. Photoshop is the choice of imaging professionals and in my opinion is the standard by which all others are measured. Photoshop is expensive and perhaps too complex for most casual users. However, if you want the best, you have this author's opinion. Adobe does make a less complicated but excellent version called Photoshop Elements CS. This version is much less expensive and at times is included free with better flatbed scanners. Other basic image-editing software programs include Kodak EasyShare, Roxio Photosuite, ArcSoft PhotoImpressions, MicroSoft PictureIt and the more advanced Jasc Paintshop Pro to name only a few.

Many photographers use image-editing software simply to fine-tune their photographic images and prepare them for printing. With a few basic adjustments in lightness/darkness, this image now has terrific visual appeal.

Editing Images

The digital realm offers incredible control in everything from eliminating a little shadow under the eyes to brightening the entire image. Image editing starts by carefully evaluating the image you are going to edit to determine what part of the image already looks great and what areas need a little help. In this next section we'll explore the principle tools of image editing.

SIZE OR SCALE Before you start to work on your digital image, it is best to adjust its size for the intended use. If you intend to use it on a scrapbook page and you want it to be 4 x 6" in size, then you must scale it accordingly. However, remember that digital images are made up of pixels and depending on how the image was created, you only have so many pixels to work with. For the best results remember this rule: Your final image should contain no more pixels than it started with. For example, if your image is 4 x 6" at 300 ppi (pixels per inch) and you double the size of the image to make it an 8 x 10" image, the resolution will be 150 ppi, or half the resolution, but the number of total pixels stays the same. What you want to avoid is "interpolation," which is the process image-editing software uses to add pixels to increase image resolution. Although many image-editing programs have very sophisticated interpolation capabilities, it is not recommended for optimum image quality and often produces images that are soft or fuzzy looking.

SHARPNESS This feature determines how "in-focus" an image appears. Most image-editing programs have a sharpness feature. This does not mean that you can correct out-of-focus images in your computer. The sharpening feature in image-editing software allows you to "emphasize" or sharpen the edge between different tonal areas. At times this is required for digital images, even in sharp focus, as the process of image editing may "soften" an image. It is possible to over-sharpen an image. An over-sharpened image looks jagged with rough edges between tones and colors.

BRIGHTNESS/CONTRAST Brightness/contrast is simply the relationship between the light areas and dark areas in an image. An image with the "correct" brightness shows detail in both the shadow and highlight areas. An image with the "correct" brightness will look neither washed out or dark and gray. Contrast is the difference between tones in an image. As a general rule, a good image will have enough contrast so that the tones separate and do not look "muddy." A more advanced method of adjusting both brightness and contrast simultaneously is by using the "levels" or "curves" command. Often image-editing programs have automatic levels and curves adjustments. However, I have found that the automatic adjustments seldom produce the results most photographers are after. If you have the option to, adjust these controls yourself.

This series of images shows how simple adjustments to sharpness and brightness/contrast can improve an image. The first image shows an original image that is too dark and not sharp enough. The second image was sharpened and the third image was adjusted for brightness and contrast. Sometimes creating a terrific final image is a matter of fine-tuning a few simple elements that can make a very big difference.

TIP: For best results, follow this simple rule: 300dpi is the optimum resolution for most printed images and 72dpi is the optimum resolution for the Internet and digital presentations.

Color Balance

This is the "Pandora's box" of image editing. Color is very subjective. When it comes to color there is no "true" color because color is created by light that is reflecting from a surface. No two light sources are exactly alike, and if we are talking about skin tone, definitely no two skin tones are alike. To better understand color in the digital environment we need to understand first how color is reproduced.

Color is reproduced using two basic methods. The first method is "additive color." In additive color red, green, and blue light are mixed to create the full spectrum of color. This is how your computer monitor works, thus it is called an RGB device. You would think that one method is good enough and we could move on, but the RGB method works for light but not for ink. So for printing devices there is another theory based on the colors cyan, magenta, yellow and black—which is referred to as CMYK color (the K stands for black). Why is this important? For most digital photographers the final image is reproduced using a color printer, so it is better to adjust color on an image that has been converted from an RGB version into a CMYK version for printing. This will result in fewer unexpected color shifts when printing the image.

Good color balance is achieved when the image has no apparent color bias. How do you tell? The next time you go to the hardware store, take a good look at the paint sample "chips" on display. Look at all of those white cards with paint color samples on them and look only at the grays. After a while you will notice that some grays have a blue cast, some have a brown cast, some look greenish, etc. The difference you see is the bias, or colorcast. Now look at a printed digital image. If it has a "bias" then it has bad color balance. The correction for a color bias is usually simple: Either subtract the color from the image (if your image looks blue remove blue) or add more of its opposite color (if your image looks blue add yellow). Blue skies, white objects and skin tones are areas where color bias or colorcast becomes most apparent.

> **TIP:** Some image-editing software programs allow you to match the image on screen to your output from your printer. This process is called "calibration." High-end image-editing software programs, like Adobe Photoshop, have software that allows you to manually calibrate your monitor. Calibrating your monitor is a good idea as it will save you time and reduce your printing costs. Calibration software can also be purchased separately.

This digital image of a young girl dressed as Cleopatra for Halloween has skin tones that are too red. The second image was color-corrected by removing red and magenta from the image and adding a little bit of yellow. Even though the brightness/contrast was not adjusted, the color corrections open up the shadow areas in her face.

Digital Image Manipulation

When many people think of photo manipulation, the first thing that comes to mind is the creation of fantastic images using the techniques of photomontage and photo collage. The truth is that photographers have been manipulating images since the birth of photography. In the 1850s, the famous photographer Oscar Gustave Reijlander combined more than one dozen negatives to produce a single image. Image-editing software makes digital image manipulation relatively easy once you have a good handle on the basics. The tools discussed in this section are not included in all image-editing programs. For the purpose of this book, I have attempted to focus on those that are most useful to photographers and scrapbookers.

WORKING IN LAYERS Layering is the single most powerful image-editing tool available. Layers work like transparent image overlays. Images can be added or altered on a layer without affecting other layers. This tool allows an image to be built in strata and if a mistake is made on one layer the layer can be deleted without affecting work on other layers. This is the ultimate software tool for creating photo collage.

ADDING TEXT TO PHOTOGRAPHS DIGITALLY

Text can be added to photographs in many image-editing software programs. However, since image-editing software is designed for images that are pixel based, often text created in these software packages looks jagged. If your software has a feature called "anti-aliasing" that will make your text look smoother. For the best results, import your image into a "vector-based" drawing program like Adobe Illustrator of Macromedia Freehand and apply your text on top of the image. Often a word-processing program such as Microsoft Word will do a better job of handling text than an image-editing program, and using the two software programs together may produce the best results.

TIP: For the cleanest and sharpest looking text when using image-editing software, use a higher resolution image. This will make for more pixels in your image and finer edge detail. This applies only if your end product is a print.

Combing two images together can create exciting visual effects. The original landscape image above was combined with the dramatic sky from the image above right. The final combination shown at right creates an image which is much more dramatic and interesting to look at.

COLOR MANIPULATION Unlike the color-correction tools discussed earlier, color manipulation tools can give an image an extreme look. My particular favorite is the "hue/saturation" tool. By changing the hue of an image, you can achieve a variety of color shifts in the image. This works well when trying to create very graphic effects. The "saturation" tool allows you to increase or decrease the color intensity of an image. A little increase in saturation may be just what an image needs, but if you continue to increase saturation the effect can be quite bold and graphic. In software programs such as Adobe Photoshop you can also use this control to "colorize" photographs.

FILTER EFFECTS Various filters are included with virtually all image-editing software. They can make your image look like a watercolor or impressionist painting, a pencil drawing or an embossed piece of metal. Using these filters is fun for unique effects on scrapbook pages, but use filters sparingly. Many software companies make filter "plug-ins" that can be purchased and added to existing image-editing software to expand your range of options.

In this work of art the layered elements of the montage have a distinctive color palette that creates cohesiveness throughout all areas of the image.

Charting a Course. Iris Print on Somerset Velvet Watercolor Paper. 1999-2000 © Angela Kelly. All rights reserved.

TIP: The beauty of digital photography is that the only limit on the number of photos you take is the memory available to you. However, if you can't find an image it will never appear on a scrapbook page. When dealing with digital images, stay organized. Always label your CDs and DVDs. Develop a protocol for naming images and files and stick to it. And print a list of the images on a CD or DVD and insert the list in the jewel case for quick reference.

Skill builder

Set aside a day or some time over a number of days to explore your image-editing software program. Choose one image to work with for the entire time. Open up your software program and begin exploring the tools. Start with color manipulation. Open up the color dialogue box or menu and select a color adjustment, then apply it to the image. Pay attention to how the image is affected by that particular adjustment. Then undo that adjustment and move on to the next adjustment. Every time you apply an effect to your image, undo that change before you move on to the next adjustment. When you have finished applying every possible color adjustment to your image, move on to filter effects. After filters, continue through every single option that your program has to offer. At the end of this skill builder you will know exactly how your images can be transformed through the software that you have. Knowing what the software can do will help you to decide exactly what you want your images to look like.

Awesome Output

Now that you have basic knowledge of color-correcting an image, properly sizing an image and removing fifteen pounds from your self-portrait, you are ready to print. Since you have made it this far and are turning into an excellent photographer you should now know the ins and outs of digital printing. In this section the assumption is made that you are printing on a color digital inkjet printer.

PRINTERS Printers, ink and paper technology have reached amazing levels. Buying a good "photo quality" printer is difficult only because there are so many good choices. In selecting a printer consider the following factors.

PRINT RESOLUTION Print resolution is measured in "dpi" or dots per inch. The higher the number, the more fine the print detail will be.

INK AND NUMBER OF INK COLORS The rule of thumb here is the more ink colors the better. More colors means better handling of subtle colors and tonal changes. The type of ink is also important. Inks come in two basic types: dye-based and pigment-based. For an explanation of the difference in ink types, see the Expert Advice on the next page. Ink and paper are expensive; compare prices if you are on a tight budget.

PRINT SPEED If you hate to wait, this is going to be a big factor in making your choice. Some printers simply print faster than others.

PAPER SIZE If all you ever want to print is an 8 x 10" print then your choice is easy; but if you want larger prints your options narrow and prices rise. Finally, always request an actual sample print from the printer you want to purchase. Different printer manufacturers make printers that place ink on the paper in different ways. Two different 1440dpi printers from two different manufacturers will make prints that look slightly different.

PRINTING PAPER Once you have selected a printer and it is loaded with ink, you have to select the proper paper. Some factors to consider are: Is the paper acid-free and archival quality? It doesn't matter if your scrapbook lasts 200 years if all the photos are faded and yellow. Do you prefer a matte or glossy surface? This is a matter of personal preference although some manufacturers make archival papers in only a few surfaces. And finally, is the paper you're using the right weight for your printer? If you like very heavy or specialty papers such as watercolor paper, make sure it will print properly and not damage your printer as it passes through.

The hot pinks and teals in this image are often tricky to reproduce in a print. To get the best possible print of an image such as this requires that you know your printer and the software you are using. The printer's manual and the manufacturer's Web site are good places for finding troubleshooting and advanced technical information. Photo: Andrea Zocchi © All rights reserved.

IN: WHAT MUST GO INTO A GOOD PRINT
- Did the original image have good exposure, composition and subject matter?
- Is the resolution of your image high enough for the quality you expect?
- Is the image sharp and color balanced?
- Is the brightness and contrast appropriately adjusted?

OUT: FACTORS THAT MAKE FOR EXCELLENT DIGITAL PRINTS
- Did you select the correct printing device (referred to as print driver) in your computer's "print" menu?
- Is your printer set to print on the paper you are using?
- Are you printing on paper that is recommended for photo-quality prints on your printer?
- Is your printer capable of the output you desire and in good working order?
- Did you let the printed image dry for the recommended time?

Expert Advice: Getting Quality Results in the Digital Realm
Barbara Kotsos, Senior Manager of Scrapbooking Solutions for Epson America, Inc.

GETTING QUALITY PRINTS

In order to produce exquisite, high-quality digital prints of treasured images, photographers need to be familiar with the features and capabilities of current color inkjet printers, their ink systems and choice of media offered by each printer manufacturer. Understanding your options and giving some thought to your expectations and the results you want to achieve with your images can help set priorities and inspire choices to enhance the look and feel of your photographs and optimize their longevity.

MATCHING PAPER TO PHOTOGRAPHIC PRINT NEEDS

Select a paper with features that meet your needs and intended use of the prints. The product's packaging usually lists key features and benefits, so take some time to make careful comparisons of paper from each manufacturer before making a selection. Photographers should also consider the image or style they want to create. For example, Epson Premium Glossy Photo Paper delivers a vibrant look that is best suited for photographers who produce portfolio prints of models, celebrities, real-estate venues and other subjects that command attention. PremierArt™ Matte Scrapbook Photo Paper for Epson helps create a soft, timeless look for archival photos of weddings or scrapbook pages that highlight special moments or occasions.

DYE-BASED VS. PIGMENT INKS

Photographers should know if their printer is equipped with a dye- or pigment-based ink system and understand the capabilities and limitations of both. Select the printer that is best-suited to meet your digital printing needs and expectations. Most manufacturers of inkjet printers calibrate their ink, media and hardware to work together as a system, optimize hardware performance and produce digital prints of exceptional quality. Epson offers several archival scrapbook photo papers for printing digital prints. When printed on PremierArt™ Matte Scrapbook Photo Paper for Epson, with genuine Epson dye- or pigment-based inks and stored in dark album conditions, digital prints can last up to 200 years.

SELECTING A PRINTER

The printer is the foundation of the digital printing system. Photographers should consider the predominant types of digital prints they will generate when selecting a printer appropriate for their needs. Epson's printers are designed and engineered to work with their premium inks and media which are specially formulated to ensure high-quality digital prints. Epson offers a wide range of printers to accommodate various sizes of digital prints ranging from 8½ x 11" and smaller to wide format prints ranging from 13" wide by 44" long. While the careful selection of hardware is essential to generating the best digital prints, photographers must also be familiar with the different types of ink and media available for their printer model so they can select the ones that create the effect and quality of output they want.

BARBARA KOTSOS is the senior manager of Scrapbooking Solutions for Epson America, Inc. Epson America, Inc. is responsible for the sales, marketing, distribution, service and support of a wide range of digital-imaging products and point-of-sale system solutions throughout the Americas. Under its brand name, Epson offers an extensive array of award-winning image-capture and image-output products, including color inkjet printers, scanners, LCD multimedia projectors and monochrome dot-matrix printers. Epson's branded products are well-suited for a broad range of customer environments including business, photography, government, education, graphic arts and the home. For more information on Epson's products, visit their Web site at www.epson.com or to locate a dealer, call 1-800-GO-EPSON.

Creative Camera Controls Simplified

It is so exciting to be able to make photographs that are exactly the way you want them to be. When you learn how to control your camera functions to achieve a certain look or feel, your photographs will be changed forever.

This chapter will show you how to use aperture to create an area of interest, make the most of shutter speeds and movement and how to use your automatic features like a pro. Knowing how to use your camera's creative controls is the most important skill that you can learn in photography.

Once you have mastered this skill, your shooting will become pure joy. You will no longer worry about whether a photograph will turn out or not but focus instead on capturing great moments and developing your own creative vision.

living HISTORY

The Littleton Historical Museum is one of our favorite "living history" farms. It's a fun place to learn how people lived and worked in Colorado in the 19th century. There are so many cool things to see and the animals are so nice and friendly!
Jake (3) and Dylan (6), October 1995

Skill builder

To see exactly how depth of field works, create a set of images that are shot from the same location using the range of aperture openings available on your camera. Scenes that have objects throughout the foreground, middle ground and background would work best. Take notes of your frame number and camera settings so that you can evaluate the images when you are finished. Don't forget that every time you change your aperture opening, your shutter speed will also have to change to create a balanced light-meter reading.

Making deliberate choices about how the depth of field looks in an image is one of the most important creative choices that a photographer can make. The shallow depth of field in this portrait accentuates the sense of wonder that a butterfly inspired in my son. The long depth of field selected for the landscape image captures a great expanse of space and gives the viewer an opportunity to see the detail and beauty that captivated my children.

Aperture and Depth of Field

One of the most powerful creative controls that you have as a photographer is to choose what areas of the scene will be sharp and what areas will be out of focus. Photographers who master the skill of choosing the areas of sharpness within each image are using the full creative potential that their cameras have to offer.

WHAT IS DEPTH OF FIELD?
The area of sharp focus within the image is called depth of field. Images with a shallow depth of field contain narrow areas of focus that can be used to turn a distracting background into a soft backdrop of color. Images with a long depth of field have sharp focus throughout the entire image area. A long depth of field can be used to give more information and detail into the photograph. Conversely, a shallow depth of field can isolate an element in your photograph making it the center of attention.

WHAT DETERMINES THE DEPTH OF FIELD?

Depth of field is determined by the size of the aperture opening. A large aperture opening will create a shallow depth of field. A small aperture opening will create a long depth of field. The set of numbers on your camera or lens that correspond to the size of the aperture openings look like this: f/2.8, f/3.5, f/4, f/5.6, f/8, f/11, f/16 and f/22. These numbers, called f-stops, identify the size of the aperture opening. In this example f/22, f/16, f/11 are the smaller aperture openings and will give you the longest depth of field while f/2.8, f/3.5 and f/4 are the larger aperture openings that will give you shallow depth of field.

HOW TO GET THE DEPTH OF FIELD YOU WANT

IN MANUAL MODE

One Consider the scene you are photographing and visualize how you want the photograph to look. Is the background interesting? Do you want it to be sharp or out of focus?

Two Determine what aperture you need to achieve the depth of field you want. A large aperture opening (f/2.8, f/3.5 and f/4) will create a shallow depth of field. A small aperture opening (f/22, f/11 and f/8) will create a long depth of field.

Three Set the aperture that you have decided to use on your camera.

Four Take a light-meter reading by pointing your camera at the scene and engaging your light meter to read the light. Do not change the aperture setting that you have already set on the camera. Instead, adjust the shutter speed so that the light meter is balanced with the aperture you have set your camera on. If you cannot arrive at a balanced reading, adjust your aperture one f-stop and repeat the process.

Five Take the photograph.

The shallow depth of field in this image creates a mountain backdrop with a "painterly" effect that focuses the viewer's attention on my son catching fish in a lake.

IN APERTURE-PRIORITY MODE

One Select the aperture-priority mode on your camera.

Two Choose the aperture you need to achieve the depth of field you want.

Three Take a light-meter reading and the camera will choose the shutter speed needed to create the correct exposure.

Four Take the photograph.

Shutter Speed and Movement

Photographers who know how to use their cameras to record and transform movement have a world of creative possibilities to pick from for every single image that they make. Cameras can record movement as stopped or blurred action giving the photograph unique visual characteristics that are unlike any other art form. Taking advantage of this unique quality will help you to create photographic images that are exciting and new.

CAPTURING MOVEMENT Movement adds a dynamic quality to photographic images. If you have a good understanding of how to control and record movement on film, you can transform a waterfall into a continuous ribbon of satin or freeze the same waterfall in a myriad of tiny water droplets suspended in space. All this is controlled by the shutter mechanism in your camera. The shutter determines how movement will appear in the image and the amount of time that light exposes the film.

A fast shutter speed stops the action of this cyclist defying gravity at a cycling demonstration event in Boston.

SHUTTER SPEEDS How movement translates onto film is determined by the speed of objects moving within the scene and the amount of time that the shutter remains open during the exposure. On your camera you will find a set of numbers that look like this: 1000, 500, 250, 125, 60, 30, 15, 8, 4, 2 and B. These numbers, called shutter speeds, identify how long the shutter will remain open. The numbers are actually fractions of time. A shutter speed of 60 is actually 1/60th of a second, 500 is actually 1/500th of a second and "B" allows the shutter to remain open as long as it is depressed. The rules for using shutter speed are simple: A fast shutter speed, 250 or higher, freezes or stops motion. Fast shutter speeds render moving objects without any blur. Slow shutter speeds, 60 or lower, will make an image appear out of focus or blurred if it is moving.

Skill builder

To see exactly how shutter speed affects movement, create a set of images that are shot from the same location using the range of shutter speeds available on your camera. Moving water is a good choice to photograph for this skill builder. Take notes of your frame number and camera settings so that you can evaluate the images when you are finished. Don't forget that every time you change your shutter speed your aperture opening will also have to change to create a balanced light-meter reading.

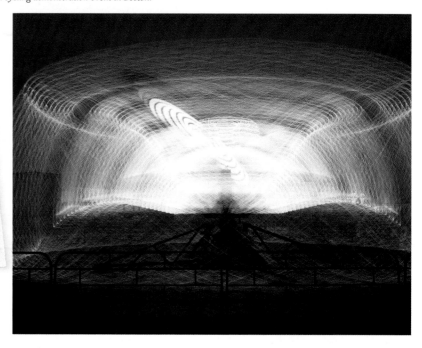

With the camera securely positioned on a tripod and a slow shutter speed, this carnival ride becomes a painting of light. The color trails created by the repeating movement of the ride over time provides an unusual and visually intriguing pattern of color.

WHEN TO USE A TRIPOD When using slow shutter speeds, you must stabilize the camera to prevent "camera shake" and unwanted blurring effects. You can stabilize your camera by using a tripod, setting the camera down on a stable surface or by bracing yourself up against a wall or tree when you are photographing. In general the camera must be stabilized with shutter speeds slower than 1/60th of a second.

HOW TO GET THE SHUTTER SPEED YOU WANT

IN MANUAL MODE

One Consider the scene you are photographing and visualize how you want the photograph to look. Do you want to stop the action of a moving object? Do you want to blur the movement of a moving object?

Two Determine what shutter speed you need in order to achieve the movement effect you desire. Again the rule is simple: A fast shutter speed will stop the action; a slow shutter speed will blur the image of a moving object.

Three Set the shutter speed to the speed you have decided to use.

Four Take a light-meter reading by pointing your camera at the scene and engaging your light meter to read the light. Do not change the shutter setting that you have already set on the camera. Instead adjust the aperture opening so that the light meter is balanced with the shutter speed that you have set your camera on. If you cannot arrive at a balanced reading, adjust your shutter one stop and repeat the process.

Five Take the photograph.

IN SHUTTER-PRIORITY MODE

One Select the shutter-priority mode on your camera.

Two Choose the shutter speed you need to achieve the movement you want to capture on film.

Three Take a light-meter reading and the camera will select the aperture needed to re-create the correct exposure.

Four Take the photograph.

A thunderstorm, captured with a camera secured on a tripod and the long-exposure mode, shows the many streaks of lightning that flashed across the sky in a short period of time.

Defying Gravity

bmx

BOSTON, MASSACHUSETTS OCTOBER 1995

After a trip to City Hall, we were fortunate to happen upon a BMX freestyle competition – which brings riders to skate parks, half-pipes, and the streets in droves. We had a great time watching the daredevils and risk-takers make their bikes and bodies do amazing things while trying to avoid the 'crash and burn'!

Automatic Features

Automatic features are terrific to have on your camera because they make difficult or unusual shooting situations easy to photograph. With auto focus you point and shoot without stopping to focus while the action passes you by. Long exposure modes will give you the courage to bring your camera to places you never thought you could. Landscape and portrait modes will help you make stunning images without having to worry about aperture or shutter-speed settings. The self-timer and remote-control modes will help you to finally get in the photograph along with the rest of your family. Once you get to know these features, you will be using them all the time because using them makes photographing a real pleasure.

AUTO FOCUS Many cameras have a convenient auto-focus function that allows you to compose and shoot your images without having to stop and focus. Most auto-focus cameras have center-weighted focusing. That is they focus on what is in the center of your viewfinder. This works well but often you will want the "in focus" part of your photograph to be off to one side. To perform this function, most auto-focus cameras have a "focus-lock" feature. Use this feature by pressing the shutter-release button halfway down and place the subject in the center of the focusing screen. Engage the auto-focus lock by depressing the shutter release halfway to set the focus distance. Without taking your finger off the shutter-release button, change your composition until you have the composition arrangement you want and take the photograph. If you take a lot of close-up photographs or shoot sports and wildlife, you will want to buy a camera that also allows you to focus the lens manually as well as automatically.

This portrait, taken in front of the stunning scenery of the Rio Grande in New Mexico, was made using the landscape mode. In the landscape mode the camera records the landscape behind the boys with great detail and depth of field. Had I made this portrait in the portrait mode, the boys would have been sharp and the background would have been out of focus.

LONG EXPOSURE OR NIGHTTIME MODE Long exposures are needed for capturing fireworks and nighttime shooting. With many cameras using the long exposure mode requires you to place your camera on a tripod and press the button that engages the long exposure mode. Then press the shutter-release button and the shutter will open and remain open for up to two minutes. At the end of the exposure, press the shutter-release button again to reset the camera.

LANDSCAPE MODE The landscape mode is identified by an icon of a mountain. This mode automatically adjusts the aperture and shutter speed of your camera to create sharp focus and a long depth of field throughout the entire scene. To use this feature simply adjust your camera to the landscape mode and point and shoot.

Skill builder

Try shooting with the long exposure mode in a variety of different situations. Remember that anything moving during a long exposure will appear as a blur and that can be a glorious visual effect. When shooting in the long-exposure mode, look for low-lighting situations. Use movement to your advantage and run with your camera during the exposure, shake things up and see what happens. Try making light drawings at night. Get a helper or two to face the camera holding a flashlight pointed at the camera lens. Slowly move the flashlight to make a "drawing" in air. Start with a 1-minute exposure then 2, 3, 4 and work your way up to a 10-minute exposure.

TIP: Instead of thinking about the landscape mode as the setting that you use to make landscape images, think of this mode as the long depth-of-field mode. Instead of photographing landscapes in this mode, try photographing people and other subjects; the results will surprise you.

The landscape mode captures a long depth of field. Sharp focus throughout the image adds detail and information to the photograph. This photograph of a villa in Italy was shot in the landscape mode to guarantee a long depth of field with sharp focus from the lilypads in the foreground to the rooftop in the background.

PORTRAIT MODE In the portrait mode the camera will adjust the aperture and shutter so that there will be a shallow depth of field or small area of sharp focus surrounded by softer focus. The portrait mode is indicated on your camera by a small portrait-silhouette icon. To use this mode set your camera to the portrait mode and point and shoot.

TIP: Instead of thinking about the portrait mode as the one used to make photographs of people, think of this mode as the shallow depth-of-field mode. Make a landscape photograph with the portrait mode and you will see how a landscape taken with a shallow depth of field can have emotive qualities.

SELF-TIMER The self-timer mode is designed to get the photographer out from behind the camera and into the photograph. This mode automatically takes the photograph ten seconds after the photographer has pushed the shutter-release button. The delay gives the photographer time to get into the photograph and to get ready for the shot. A blinking red light or an audible beep counts down the time before the photograph will be taken. To use this mode you need to have your camera stabilized on a tripod or other stable object in the scene.

REMOTE CONTROL A remote-control unit allows you to take the photograph from a distance away from the camera. The camera needs to be set on the remote-control mode; sometimes this operation is simply included in the self-timer mode on your camera. Once you have set the mode to operate your remote control, you have five minutes to take the photograph before the camera resets back to a standard operating mode. Stabilize your camera on a tripod or stable object and arrange the composition you desire. Take your remote control in hand and when you see an interesting moment unfolding before the camera, simply point the remote control unit at the receiver on the camera and the shot will be taken in two seconds.

Photographing in the portrait mode captures a shallow depth of field that creates a wash of color and tone behind the main subject. The shallow depth of field in these two images helps to separate and isolate the main subject from confusing backgrounds.

TIP: With portraiture, the moment the photographer puts the camera up to his or her eye the connection between the photographer and the subject is lost. At family gatherings, the moment you pick up the camera everyone knows that you are going to take a photograph and they all get ready to give you the expected and not very interesting "cheese" smile. Using the self-timer mode or remote control will give you the option to step away from the camera while shooting or to capture more natural moments.

How to Hold a Camera Properly

You can reduce the occurrence of "soft" or out-of-focus images by holding your camera properly. Keep your arms and elbows tucked into your body to create a stable "platform" for your camera. Stand with your legs shoulder-width apart forming a triangle with your entire body. To add more support to your standing position, lean against a doorway or something solid whenever possible. Kneel down with one knee on the ground and the other knee will become the support for your elbow, arm and camera. These techniques are most important to use when you are shooting with slow shutter speeds, such as 1/60th of a second or slower.

PREVENTING UNWANTED BLUR It is very easy to miss a memorable moment because the photograph you made came out too blurry to use. In many cases the cause of blurry images is camera shake. You can reduce the number of images lost to unwanted movement by knowing when to stabilize your camera and how to hold it properly by hand.

LENS AND SHUTTER SPEED If you are going to hand-hold your camera, you should never shoot with a shutter speed that is slower than the length of your lens without using a support to stabilize the camera. If you are shooting with a 50mm lens you should not shoot below a 1/60th shutter speed while handholding the camera. If you are using a 75mm or 80mm lens do not shoot below 1/125th without support. If you are using a long lens or have your zoom lens adjusted to 200mm you should not shoot with a shutter speed slower than 1/250th without support.

STABILIZING YOUR CAMERA I have stabilized my camera on everything from fence posts and chairs to the hood of my car and the crook of a tree. By placing your camera down on something stable you can reduce camera shake and shoot with shutter speeds even slower than those recommended for use with the lens. If you have a self-timer on your camera you can further reduce camera shake by engaging the self-timer to trip the shutter while your camera is sitting on a stable object. Using the self-timer will reduce any movement that can occur from the act of depressing the shutter release button.

Create a triangle shape with your body: legs apart and arms in tight against your torso.

This series of images shows a variety of ways to stabilize your camera as you hold it. Good form while photographing will reduce the potential for camera shake that results in blurred, unusable images.

Crouch down and use your own knee as a tripod.

TIP: If you must hand-hold your camera at a slow shutter speed, take a deep breath, let the air out and then shoot. You will get less camera shake than when trying to hold your breath while you take the shot.

Stabilize or brace yourself on objects near you, such as this bridge railing.

Expert Advice: Getting Controls to Work in Unison

Ken Trujillo, Photography Studio Manager, F+W Publications—Denver Office

SHUTTER SPEED AND APERTURE WORKING IN UNISON

Anyone can take a photograph with the camera set on automatic and get a reasonably well-exposed image. However, there will be times when your camera will not know how to handle a situation; good knowledge of shutter speed and aperture can help. To really understand exposure, you need to know how shutter speed and aperture work together. Understanding this relationship will help you make better exposures and will help you to be more creative.

APERTURE CAN DETERMINE SHUTTER SPEED

If your camera allows you to shoot in a manual mode, aperture-priority mode or shutter-priority mode, you will be able to take advantage of your shutter speed and aperture settings. When considering what aperture setting to photograph with, determine what you want in focus and what you want to be the main focal point in the image. Sometimes choosing an aperture setting is a question of deciding what you don't want in an image, like a cluttered background. For me, the shutter-speed setting is often predetermined by the aperture setting that I want to use in the photograph. If I want a shallow depth of field in the image, I will likely have to photograph with a faster shutter-speed setting. If I want a long depth of field in an image then I will probably have to choose a slower shutter-speed setting for the image.

EXPERIMENT AND PRACTICE

If you want to learn how to make more deliberate and thoughtful choices about how your images look, experiment with many different ways to shoot a single image. Take your camera and go shoot for fun. Shoot some close-up shots with a large aperture opening to get a shallow depth of field. Shooting as close as you can will help you see how a large aperture takes the background out of focus. Try shooting along a fence and change your focus in each shot from the front to middle to back while using a large aperture opening, then see what happens when you take the same shots with a small aperture opening.

To practice with your shutter-speed settings, attend a youth sporting event. Try to capture the fast action with both fast and slow shutter-speed settings. Try using a slow shutter speed as you pan along with a moving subject. A playground is another great place to experiment with shutter-speed settings. Take photographs of your kids on swings or merry-go-rounds as you experiment with a variety of shutter-speed settings. Practice does make perfect, and the only real way to understand how shutter speed and aperture work together is to give it a try.

KEN TRUJILLO runs the photography studio for F+W Publications, Inc.'s Denver division producing best-selling magazines and books. Married with two daughters, Mercedes and Parris, he and his wife Julie live in Thornton, Colorado. A graduate of the Colorado Institute of Art in 1997, he earned his degree in photography. Shortly after graduating he opened his own commercial photography studio in Denver's historic Union Station. Working for both national and local clients, he built a successful business and won several awards for his advertising photography. Since 2000, Ken has been staff photographer for the publishers of Memory Makers magazines and books. In the last five years he has helped facilitate their growth into a fully digital studio and taken their yearly production from nine projects in 2000 to thirty-six in 2004.

Break. Digital Quadtone Print. © Ken Trujillo.

Working With Light

Light is ever changing. In one day the light can shift from warm to cool, hard to soft, or flat to raking. Light is the paint on the photographer's palette. Light sets the mood of the image, establishes the time of day and defines how the subject will look.

Photographers who have a sophisticated understanding of light and the technical skills to control the light can create expressive images that move the viewer and transform the scene in unexpected ways.

In this chapter you will learn how to see light in new ways and how to capture, control, and modify the light to create beautiful images. As you become more sensitive to the wonderful qualities of light and start using the skills presented in this chapter, I have no doubt that your photographic images will dazzle everyone.

The dramatic qualities of hard light can be used to make visually powerful images. When photographing hard-light conditions, be sure to check your light-meter reading carefully as the extreme contrast in the scene can cause exposure problems. Photo: Andrea Zocchi © All rights reserved.

Beautiful Natural Light

Photographers who know how to identify and use natural light to create images have a world of possibilities to choose from. The "quality" of light is so important that many photographers spend hours waiting for the light to change in just the right way before taking the photograph. Natural light is full of identifiable characteristics—such as color, softness, clarity and direction—that when thoughtfully rendered in a photograph can be used to imply meaning and elicit emotion.

COLOR OF LIGHT The color of light shifts throughout the day as the sun rises and sets. In early morning and late afternoon the light is usually warm with a red, yellow or orange glow. This is superb light to photograph in and is well worth getting up early or rearranging your late-day schedule for. At other times of the day, such as between 10 a.m. and 3 p.m., light can be cool and blue in color. Choosing to shoot in warm or cool light is a choice that you should consciously make as it will influence the emotive feel of the image. Warm light is soothing and inviting while cool light lends a chilly aura to a photographic image.

The golden glow of a setting sun is worth waiting for as it can turn an ordinary scene into an embracing spectrum of colors.

Fog creates an ethereal quality of light and a wide variety of subtle gray tones with splashes of color in between.

QUALITY OF LIGHT On overcast days light is "soft" because the sun's rays are diffused through the clouds and scatter across the scene from many different angles. Soft light creates open shadows and reduces the amount of contrast in a scene. Photographs made in soft light are easier to expose accurately because the range of color tones is narrower and well within the contrast range that photographic film and digital pixels can capture easily. Colors in soft light appear more vibrant and rich. Soft light can be used to create a melancholy or romantic feel in your images.

"Hard" light is dramatic and full of contrast. Because it is light that comes from one light source, harsh shadows will be present that can be used to create visually dynamic compositions. Sometimes hard light is so intense that it can wash out the color in an image and create unwanted glare. Hard light is more difficult to expose accurately because it often contains a wide contrast range that is difficult for film and digital pixels to record. When captured carefully, images made in hard light can feel full of energy and emotionally intense.

DIRECTION OF LIGHT Direct lighting is when the direction of the light comes from behind the photographer and falls on the front of the subject. With this kind of lighting, the subject is well lit but harsh shadows behind the subject might appear causing the image to look flat or two-dimensional. Glare is often pronounced as it bounces off of reflective surfaces. Direct light in portraiture can result in squinted eyes. When creating a portrait in direct, light ask the subject to close his or her eyes while you count to three. On the count of three the subject opens his or her eyes and you release the shutter; this sometimes helps to reduce squinting. Direct light is easy to photograph but not often the best choice for flattering results when photographing people.

SIDE LIGHTING Side lighting occurs when the light source strikes the subject from the side. When the light rakes across the surface of the subject, the three-dimensional qualities are pronounced as distinct shadows and illuminated highlights define depth and detail. Side light can provide stark contrast and requires careful light-meter readings for proper exposure. In portraiture, side lighting can be used to create dramatic portraits. In landscape images, side lighting helps to define the depth within a space.

BACK LIGHTING Backlighting is when the light source is coming from behind the subject with the photographer facing the subject. If the light source is very bright and the photographer uses the recommended light-meter reading, a silhouetted image will occur. Contrast is often so extreme that the camera simply cannot capture detail in both the highlights and the shadow areas. In the next chapter, I will show you how to use backlighting to achieve exciting images.

TOP LIGHTING Top lighting comes from a light source hitting the top of your subject. In the middle of a sunny day, top lighting is at its peak. Photographing under these lighting conditions results in images that are flat with short shadows and bright highlights. Portraits made in top lighting are usually void of any detail in the eyes as the forehead and brow will cast a dark shadow in the eye sockets and the chin will cast a dark shadow on the neck. It is best to avoid this kind of light for portraiture.

Direct light is brilliant with plenty of light for excellent exposures. Portraits created in direct light require a willing subject who can endure the intense light without squinting.

Side lighting accentuates texture, detail and depth. The side lighting created by the raking afternoon light sets the mood for a summer evening feast of fresh vegetables, cheese, bread and wine.

Skill builder

Photograph the same exact scene at different times of day from sunrise through sunset. It is amazing how significantly light changes throughout the day and how it affects photographs.

The top lighting of this river scene creates a wash of autumn colors reflecting off the surface of the water.

Electrifying Flash

Electronic flash is a portable lighting unit that can be used as the primary light source or as additional lighting to enhance the available light. Whether you are shooting indoors or out, with black-and-white or color film, knowing how to use a flash can expand your creative options and make impossible lighting situations work for you.

FLASH BASICS Flash units can be built into the camera, attached directly to the camera via a "hot shoe" or connected by a cable called a "sync cord." Flash units function by building a charge that is stored in the capacitor. When the capacitor is fully charged the flash unit's ready light glows green. When the flash is fired, the light emitted from the flash lasts for a short duration in time, usually from 1/1000th to 1/40,000 of a second. Flash units are designed to fire at the exact moment that your shutter slides fully open in the camera. After the flash fires, it begins to build up the energy it will need for the next shot; this is called the flash's "recycle time."

FLASH AND SYNC SPEED Because the flash is designed to fire at the exact moment that the shutter fully opens, a shutter speed that coincides with the light output must be used when shooting with a flash. The shutter speed must synchronize with the flash output. Most cameras synchronize with the flash at 1/60th or 1/125th of a second. Synchronization or sync speeds are often a different color on your shutter speed dial than the other shutter speeds. A lightning-bolt icon next to the appropriate shutter-speed number could also indicate the sync speed. Using a shutter speed that is faster than the indicated sync speed will result in images that are partially exposed. Using a shutter speed that is slower than the indicated sync speed may result in a ghosting effect called "slow-curtain synchronization."

Flash can be used as the primary light source (below) or combined with ambient light (left) to fill light into dark shadow areas. Knowing how to use a flash in a variety of lighting situations will expand your potential to make amazing photographs in every lighting situation you encounter.

TIP: Intriguing visual effects can be created with a slow shutter speed and flash in combination. If you set your shutter speed slower than the sync speed and use a flash, you will get an image that is sharp where the flash stopped the action and blurred in the rest of the image. This technique is easy to do once you get the hang of it. Give it a bit of practice and start using it to photograph dance parties, a night out on the town, a sporting event or the nonstop energy of your toddler.

FLASH AND RED EYE Red eye, or pupils that glow red, is caused by the flash bouncing off the retinal blood vessels in the back of your subject's eyes. In low light and dark situations red eye is often a problem because the pupil is fully dilated. To reduce red eye, increase the ambient light in the room, do not have the subject look directly into the lens of the camera or bounce the flash off the ceiling or a nearby wall. If you have a camera with a red-eye-reduction feature, be sure to use it.

Flash is terrific to use in low-lighting situations to bring out missing details in the scene. In low-lighting situations using a flash can be the difference between a perfectly exposed image and an image that is unusable. Without the addition of a flash, this photograph of a wine cellar would not have had enough light to photograph.

FLASH TYPES This section will discuss accessory flash units or flash units that are not built in to your camera. These units can be divided into two types: the dedicated flash and the manual/automatic flash. The dedicated flash unit is usually made by the manufacturer of the camera and is designed to work in the hot shoe of your camera or with a special dedicated cable. It can "communicate" with your camera, taking advantage of your camera's automatic modes and often works with your camera's auto focus and metering systems. These flash units give you added flash power and often allow you to do creative effects like "slow-curtain synchronization." With slow-curtain synchronization a photographer can shoot with a combination of flash and slow shutter speeds. The slow shutter speed will keep the shutter open for a longer amount of time than it takes for the flash to fire. The output of light coming from the flash will illuminate and stop the action of objects moving within the scene while the shutter remains open capturing additional ambient light and movement. The resulting images show movement that is stopped sharp and bright by the flash in some areas and blurred by the slow shutter speed in other areas.

The second type of accessory flash is a manual/automatic unit. This non-dedicated unit connects to your camera via the hot shoe or with a sync cable. It does not take advantage of the sophisticated automatic functions of many newer cameras but still performs well. These units usually cost less than the dedicated units and are ideal for all manual cameras. You should know that using a flash unit that is not compatible with the camera's electronic system can damage many of today's cameras—both film and digital. Always check your camera owners manual before attaching any accessory flash to the camera.

Fill flash is fantastic to use in portraiture. The flash output fills facial features with light, reduces harsh shadows and adds a flattering look to every individual.

Combining Flash & Natural Light

Mixing flash and natural light together can create fabulous results. The flash can be used as a secondary light source to sunlight and will serve to fill deep shadow areas with light. As flash units become more sophisticated, the use of flash and natural light together is becoming easier to do all the time.

HOW TO USE FILL FLASH Often ambient light does not allow you to create the photograph you would like. In many of these situations, fill flash can give your photograph that extra light needed to turn it from flat to fantastic. In fill-flash mode your flash emits just enough light to balance the ambient or existing light. Better cameras with built-in flash also allow you to vary the output of your fill flash, and this feature is worth every extra dollar you might spend, particularly on a digital camera. Many manual/automatic flashes have fill-flash capability as well; you should refer to your flash manual to determine how fill-flash functions on these units work. Follow these simple tricks to adjust your fill-flash output:

One Cover your flash with tissue paper or white vellum. The paper will reduce and soften the light. If you want to use this technique, be sure to try it on a number of images of the same scene and vary your exposure. Also try different densities of paper or vellum for more or less softness.

Two If you can adjust the angle of your flash head, try bouncing the light from your flash off the ceiling, a wall or other nearby object to reduce the flash output in the scene. Remember that by increasing your distance from flash to subject, you can reduce flash output. Pointing your camera at the ceiling or the wall will increase the distance your flash will have to travel, thereby reducing the flash output. Bouncing your flash off of other surfaces can greatly benefit your images by creating more natural-looking light and reducing the harsh shadows that can occur behind a subject when you point the flash directly at it. A warning: White walls and ceilings work best. A green wall will reflect green light.

Skill builder

Spend a day shooting with your flash. Shoot a number of images with your flash as the primary light source. To create this effect, shoot in a low-light situation. Then experiment with using your flash as fill light. Look for a bright lighting situation and use flash to fill in the shadow areas of the subject. Make notes of your camera's settings and the flash settings. When you get the film back, evaluate the results.

In backlit situations, a flash can be used to create a balanced exposure between the bright background and any objects in the foreground. Without a flash this image would have been a silhouette. With a flash, detail is captured throughout the scene.

Difficult Lighting Situations

In an evenly lit scene, the camera's recommended settings will work beautifully to achieve the perfect exposure. But photographers often face difficult lighting situations that require the photographer to override the camera's recommended reading. Difficult lighting situations can result in extremely dramatic and exciting images. Understanding how to identify a difficult lighting situation and knowing the steps that you need to take to create a fantastic exposure will allow you to photograph in every lighting situation that you come across.

Skill builder

Find a few difficult lighting situations and practice making better exposures. Take a light-meter reading of the scene, adjust your camera's recommended settings and take the shot. Then identify the darkest areas of the scene, the lightest areas of the scene and areas that have an average amount of light. Take a light-meter reading in the average lighting area by filling the frame with this area. Adjust your camera's settings to create a perfect exposure in this area. Then compose an image of the entire scene and take the shot. Evaluate the film to see how your first shot compares to the second shot. Doing this exercise will help you build great exposure skills as you begin to identify what areas in the scene you should use to take your light-meter readings in.

IDENTIFYING DIFFICULT LIGHTING The most challenging lighting situations to expose properly are high-contrast scenes and single-color scenes. Typical high-contrast situations include an interior scene with bright sunlight streaming through a window, a landscape that has a dark foreground and a bright sky or a city street with dark buildings in shadow and shafts of bright light slicing through the space. Typical single-color scenes include a snowy landscape or an ocean scene where water meets sky.

HIGH CONTRAST The challenge of a high-contrast scene is the extreme range of light to dark in the image. If you use the recommended light-meter reading for a high-contrast scene, you will get an image that has either superb details and a full range of tones in the highlight areas—with dark areas that have no detail—or great details and a full range of tones in the dark areas and bright hot white areas in the highlights that have no details. The only way to accommodate these extreme conditions is to be very careful about where you take a light-meter reading. Find an area in the scene that does not have the extreme of bright light or low light. Look for any area that has a middle-gray tone. Take a light-meter reading in the middle-gray area and your exposure will be more accurate. Another technique is to average the highlights and the shadow areas. To experiment with averaging of highlights and shadows, try this:

One Take a light-meter reading in the bright areas of the scene and note the recommended aperture and shutter-speed reading—for example, 1/60th at f/22.

Two Set your camera on either the aperture or shutter-speed reading of the first exposure and take a second light-meter reading in the dark areas of the scene—for example, 1/60th at f/5.6.

Three Determine the average aperture opening between the two aperture settings—for example, f/11, which is in the middle of the f-stops (f/22, f/16, f/11, f/8, f/5.6).

Four Keep your shutter speed at 1/60th and set your aperture to f/11; then take the shot.

Single-Color Scenes

Snow is always difficult to photograph. Recommended light-meter readings are designed to produce a middle gray tone on the film or pixels. If you point your camera at a snowy field and use the recommended light-meter reading, you will get gray snow. If you point your camera at a dark wall and use the recommended light-meter reading, you will get a gray wall. The only way to accommodate these situations is to use a gray card or to override the recommended light-meter reading. There is no need to carry around a gray card with a digital camera because you can see your results as you shoot and readjust the exposure to get the perfect image.

GRAY CARD Use an 18%-gray card, which can be purchased at your local camera store. Your camera's light meter is designed to create an exposure that will transform the light into an average shade between black and white called middle gray. Most lighting situations will record with a full tonal range but with single-color scenes or difficult lighting situations the photographer has to override the camera. An 18%-gray card will allow you to get much closer to an excellent exposure in unusual lighting situations. Try these steps for getting the best exposure possible using a gray card:

One Identify an area of the scene that has average light with no extreme light or dark areas.

Two Place the gray card in that exact area, or an area closer to you that has the same lighting conditions.

Three Look through the camera and fill the entire frame with the gray card.

Four Take a light-meter reading of the gray card and adjust your camera as recommended.

Five Keep these exposure settings, remove the gray card, compose your image and shoot.

EXPOSURE ADJUSTMENTS WITHOUT GRAY CARD

One Take a light-meter reading of the scene and note the recommended aperture and shutter-speed combination.

Two To photograph a snowy scene, adjust either the shutter speed or aperture opening to allow more light into the camera and take additional shots with varying degrees of adjustment. Increase your aperture by two f-stops (f/11 to f/5.6) or slow your shutter speed down (1/500th to 1/125th) and take the shot.

Three To photograph a dark scene, adjust either the shutter speed or aperture opening to reduce the amount of light coming into the camera and take additional shots with varying degrees of adjustment. Decrease your aperture by two f-stops (f/8 to f/16) or quadruple your shutter speed (1/60th to 1/250th) and take the shot.

Once you get used to finding it, 18% gray is everywhere. In the color of a wall, faded blue jeans and grass. If you don't have a gray card, find something gray in the scene to take a light meter reading of. The greenish-blue door of this building was a nearly perfect 18% gray.

The Colorado blizzard of March 2003 turned our back yard into a winter wonderland. With every photograph I compensated the recommended light-meter reading by adding more light in the exposure to guarantee that the snow would reproduce as white and not gray.

Snow stunts

March 17, 2003. Colorado saw one of the biggest snow storms in over 100 years! The whole front range saw something like 4 to 5 feet of snow over 5 days. When the snow was over and the drifts big enough, Marco and Luca could not resist going outside to sled down the drifts that formed along our fence. We could not resist getting these pictures of the two of them playing in the snow.

Expert Advice: It's All About the Light

Stephen Tourlentes, Visiting Associate Professor of Photography, Massachusetts College of Art

PHOTOGRAPHS THAT SPEAK FOR THEMSELVES

The biggest disappointment when photographing is having to explain how great the photograph-making moment was rather than having the image relay that to the viewer. Usually this means that you have to be there to explain your photographs rather than letting them "speak" for themselves. Spend the time to thoroughly observe your subject and study the light. It is the foundation on which your photographs are built.

IT'S ALL ABOUT LIGHT

I try to repeat this when I'm about to make a photograph: "It's the light, dummy!" The way light falls on your subject can make or break the image. Getting up early and catching the first light of day gives you a much different quality of natural light compared to noonday sun. You can convey a different mood simply by returning to a location and photographing it at different times of the day. Sometimes the subtraction of light from a scene is more important than adding light. Night photography is a good example: A place lit by the sun in the daytime is suddenly dramatically different when dimly lit at night by electric lights from multiple sources. A good tripod can bring new possibilities to your images by allowing you to use long time exposures to record dimly lit scenes.

EXTRA EXPOSURES

Surprise yourself and don't skimp on making extra exposures—often extra exposures of the subject in a variety of lighting situations, from different angles and camera settings, will lead you to more creative images. I find that I'm often initially inspired to make an image but it's usually the extra exposure that was not part of my original plan that ends up being the interesting image. By making the extra exposures, you are studying your subject in a way that goes beyond your original expectations. This also gives you more images to choose from when you begin to edit your photographs.

RE-CREATE WHAT YOU SEE

Finally, the best advice I can give you is to go to your local library or museum and look at their collection of photography books and images. Look at photographs that are filled with great light. Consider how the light was created and how the photographer chose to capture it. Try re-creating what you see in your own images. The history of the photographic medium is fascinating, and inspiration is the first step in the photograph-making process.

STEPHEN TOURLENTES currently teaches and works as a visiting associate professor of photography at the Massachusetts College of Art in Boston and The Island Center for the Arts in Skopelos, Greece. He has been a contributing editor to Blindspot Magazine since 1999. His work is held in many photographic collections, and he is a recipient of many awards including a Guggenheim Fellowship in photography.

King and Queen of the Mardi Gras. 8 x 10" Silver Print.
© Stephen Tourlentes. All rights reserved.

Visual Dynamics:
Giving Your Photographs Impact

There is a big difference between taking a photograph and making a photograph. Taking a photograph implies a snapshot—the recording of a fleeting moment captured by the photographer. It suggests a lack of control or thoughtful consideration of how the image should look. Making a photograph implies deliberate choices made in constructing a photograph.

In this chapter you will learn how to make photographs with visual impact rather than simply taking them and hoping for the best. You will learn how to use composition, subject matter, color, texture, point of view, reflections, framing, scale and special lighting effects to energize the composition of your photographs.

Leading photographers use visual dynamics to make us laugh, surprise us, shock us and change our perception of the world. With practice, careful observation and thoughtful choices, you will be making photographs that transform the ordinary into the extraordinary in no time at all.

The way to experience a new place is to put the map away and take whatever turn in the road that looks the most inviting. While driving through the Italian countryside I came upon this ancient church. The passing of time had left

The "rule of thirds" applies to both horizontal and vertical images. Using this compositional strategy will guarantee terrific compositions every time.

Composition

To create a terrific composition, the photographer has to make decisions about how to put the photograph together. Should the horizon line be in the middle of the frame or at the bottom? Should the image be vertical or horizontal? Should the subject matter be placed in the middle or off center? To make dynamic compositions, artists organize visual elements in deliberate ways with the goal of creating pathways through the image that guide the viewer's eye. Understanding these strategies and incorporating them into your photographic practices will help you to improve every image that you make.

RULE OF THIRDS
The "rule of thirds," developed by artisans many centuries ago, is a tool for creating well-balanced compositions. The rule is simple: Imagine a grid of lines placed over your viewfinder that divides your image into nine equal rectangles. By centering the main subject of your photograph at any of the four intersecting lines of the grid, you will have created a more dynamic composition. The rule of thirds helps you place your subject or point of interest at a location in the frame where there is dynamic tension between the subject and the rest of the image.

HORIZONTAL VS. VERTICAL
Choosing horizontal or vertical framing for your composition will depend upon the subject matter you are photographing. For vertical subject matter—like tall buildings, waterfalls and flowers—vertical framing will capture the entire object and help to fill the frame. For horizontal subject matter—like landscapes, swimming pools and large groups—horizontal framing is an appropriate choice. The best way to choose which framing format works best for the subject is to try them both. Look through the viewfinder and compose the image horizontally, then recompose the same image holding your camera vertically. Decide which image has the most dynamic composition. The key point here is to see how it looks in both formats and to make a deliberate decision as to which one works best. Too often amateur photographers neglect to turn the camera resulting in poor composition.

Skill builder

Find an interesting scene that you can make many images of. Take ten or more images of that scene while standing in the same area. Work hard to make every single frame a different and unique composition. This skill builder will help you fine-tune your ability to identify and create exciting compositions. Sometimes simply crouching down to photograph makes all the difference in the world.

The decision to create a vertical or horizontal composition of any scene should start with looking through the camera to see what both versions look like. The vertical composition of this church on the Big Island of Hawaii creates better proportions and fills the frames more effectively than the horizontal version.

CONSIDER THE ENTIRE FRAME
Often inexperienced photographers place their subjects right in the middle of a horizontal image and forget to pay attention to the rest of the photograph. Great compositions require the photographer to consider the center and everything else in the frame including the top, the bottom, the left side and the right side. Keep in mind that every part of the image is important and look for ways to fill the entire frame with visual elements that support and enhance the entire composition. Usually the first time we bring the camera to our eye we frame the subject in the center. To add more to the composition, move closer until the subject fills the frame. Try moving around the subject and observe how elements in the background can be used to enhance the composition. Try moving the subject to make the most of the visual potential within the space you are photographing.

Creating a great portrait is often a matter of taking five steps closer to your subject and filling the entire frame with those wonderful smiles that are so contagious.

FOREGROUND, MIDDLE GROUND AND BACKGROUND
A photographic image is a two-dimensional interpretation of a three-dimensional space. To create the illusion of depth and to direct the viewer's eye throughout the composition, photographers must consider the visual elements of foreground, middle ground and background. Objects placed in the foreground can be used to establish scale and to draw the viewer's attention toward a particular part of the scene. Great photographers use visual elements such as line, shape and color to direct the viewer's attention from the foreground to the middle ground in the image. The middle ground is often the primary focal point that highlights or identifies the subject matter of the photograph. The background can be used to establish the place, to serve as a backdrop for the primary subject, to establish depth within the space or to add information that helps define the subject. When composing your images, pay close attention to the foreground, middle ground and background and use these visual elements to add new dimension to your photographs.

TIP: If you have the luxury of time to create an image, take a few moments to see all the possible arrangements that you can make. Look through your camera and walk around the scene. Arrange the image in a variety of ways. Once you have explored the scene though your camera, decide which arrangement was the most dynamic and go back to shoot it.

Making careful choices about the placement of objects in the foreground, middle ground and background is important as these elements create a visual pathway through the image creating a dynamic experience for the viewer.

The horizon line placed at the top of the frame accentuates deep space in the image and creates a solitary and contemplative mood.

HORIZON LINE
Putting the horizon line in the exact center of the photograph will result in a composition that is anything but dynamic. To become more inventive with horizon line placement, use the rule of thirds as a guideline for putting your images together. Consider the scene you are photographing and make a number of photographs using the rule of thirds as your starting point. Placing the horizon line within the top one-third of the image will emphasize the middle ground and foreground of the scene. Placing the horizon line in the bottom one-third of the image will emphasize the sky. Try pushing it even further by composing images with just a sliver of information at the very bottom of the image or position the horizon line at the very top of the photograph. These seemingly simple changes can be the difference between a boring image and a really terrific one.

The sharp angles and bold colors of these cigar boats create a wonderfully dramatic image that implies speed and power.

ANGLES AND CURVES
Every object or place has angles or curves that you can use to increase the visual drama of your photographs. Turning these elements into great compositions begins with recognizing their visual potential. In your photographs, roadways could become ribbons of light that meander like a river through the scene. The vertical slats of a rocking chair can become a terrific hard-edged backdrop that emphasizes the soft curves of a child's face. Before you even make the photograph, take a good look at the scene. Look for curves and angles in the objects around you and in the spaces where you are photographing. Take advantage of these graphic visual elements to compose the image. Then look through the viewfinder and walk around the scene to see how these elements change with your position. When the compositional elements come together in exciting ways, make the photograph.

FRAME-WITHIN-A-FRAME
A fabulous compositional strategy is to create a frame-within-a-frame around the image. When objects and architectural elements are transformed into framing devices that surround the subject matter, the viewer's attention goes directly to the subject of the photograph. Creating a frame-within-a-frame can also add harmony, balance and visual interest to your photographs. Framing devices are all around us, and finding interesting ones to use is simply a matter of how observant you are and how creative you can be. Once you start paying attention to interesting framing opportunities and begin using them in your images, your imagination will take over and all of a sudden you will see a world filled with frames just waiting for you to use.

TIP: Consider constructing your own frames for a frame-within-a-frame shot. Find a beautiful old frame at a yard sale and use it to create a portrait of your best friend. Create a 2 x 2' scrapbook page and cut an opening out that you can shoot through then set your kids up behind the opening and make a portrait of them. If you are shooting next to a tree, have a helper pull a tree branch down into the scene so it surrounds your subject while you shoot.

Architectural elements such as doorways, arches and windows can be used as framing devices that surround the subject and fill the frame with interesting visual elements.

Color

It is amazing how color influences our perception and interpretation of the world. Have you ever noticed how some people dress in pastel colors while others choose narrow palettes of muted tones? The colors that we dress in, paint our living rooms with and choose for our scrapbook pages tell us something about our personalities. Bright colors are outgoing, playful and distinct. Muted colors are somber, contemplative and serious. There are many renowned artists and works of art that are famous for their extraordinary use of color. Paying close attention to color and how you use it in your photographs will help you create mood and emotion in your images.

DOMINANT COLOR When you find yourself in a situation that has one dominant color, take advantage of it because dominant-color images are very dramatic. Dominant-color images can be created when paying close attention to the light source that illuminates a scene. As the sun sets, warm light covers everything in its path in pinks, yellows, oranges and reds while shadows in the snow become a cold, bright blue and candlelight is golden and romantic. Dominant colors can also be found in architecture such as a brightly painted wall, or in nature against a background of a red cliff. To create a successful dominant-color image, be sure to isolate the color so that you will achieve the most dramatic results. Dominant-color images are often most effective when simple and minimal in composition.

COLOR HARMONY Unlike complementary colors, harmonic colors are grouped next to each other on the color wheel, like purple and blue, blue and green, green and yellow, yellow and orange and orange and red. The effects of color harmony can be pronounced when the colors are muted, have the same intensity or when no complementary colors are present. Color harmony creates a calming effect, implies simplicity and suggests nature. Weather effects can create a wide range of color harmony. Fog, rain and overcast days diffuse color intensity and narrow the range of colors in a scene. You can create color harmony by doing simple things like choosing the clothes that your subject wears, pulling a curtain closed or moving your subject from in front of a contrasting background to a more harmonious background.

Color affects our emotions and influences our understanding of the world. Creating photographs that isolate one or two dominant colors will help to give your images greater emotional impact.

Paying close attention to color relationships can lead to fantastic images. The yellow-orange pumpkins placed in front of a bright-blue door create a dynamic contrast of color.

COLOR CONTRAST Contrasting colors, also called complementary colors, are colors that are opposite each other on the color wheel. When opposite colors are combined together, they create visual tension that heightens the impact of photographic images. Juxtaposing contrasting colors next to each other will have both a physical and psychological effect. Look for these contrasting color combinations the next time you go out to photograph: yellow and blue, red and green, orange and purple or warm and cool and bright and muted. These dynamic combinations can be used to imply young and old, soft and hard, quiet and loud, open and closed, happy and sad, vibrant and dull, passive and aggressive and strong and weak.

Point of View

Many photographers shoot standing up with their cameras held at eye level. When a photographer shoots this way all the time, all of his or her images begin to look alike because the point of view is always the same. It is amazing what can happen to your photographs when you break that bad habit and start seeing the world from other points of view.

PHOTOGRAPHING FROM BEHIND Some of the favorite photographs that I have made of my two boys have been taken from behind. They often walk holding hands or stand arm in arm. My interest in photographing them from behind is not to create a descriptive photograph but to make an image that captures the sweetness of that gesture and the closeness that they share with each other. We all understand and know how most things look from the front because that is the way we see than most of the time. Shooting from behind presents the photographer and the viewer with a visual landscape that is new and interesting.

The point of view in this image reinforces the feeling of an endless sea just waiting to be explored.

GET UP AND LOOK DOWN I have known plenty of photographers who have climbed trees just to shake up the vantage point, and I must admit that I have done it myself. Photographing from up above the subject can change the relationship of everything—the ground becomes the background, the space compresses and objects can appear smaller or more significant. When you have the opportunity to shoot from a higher vantage point, you are likely to create more interesting images because the point of view transforms the subject matter in unexpected ways. Here are some ideas for getting up higher, but always keep in mind that safety comes first—no photograph is worth a broken leg or worse. Try photographing from the bed of a truck, a bridge, a high window, a hillside or an elevator with glass windows. A stable ladder or step stool is an invaluable tool especially for group portraits or for photographs of people seated around a table.

GET DOWN AND LOOK UP Put yourself in somebody else's shoes. Imagine what the world looks like from your toddler's point of view. She has to look up to see most of her world. Imagine what the world looks like from an ant's point of view: a blade of grass is a bridge, a rock is a mountain and a tree is a magic beanstalk. Portraits made from a low vantage point can turn an individual into a hero. Looking up will surprise you. A canopy of trees can become a quilt of dappled light. Your sweet cat can become a menacing feline on the prowl. The mountain-bike rider can become a rocket hurling through space. Lie down on the grass and photograph that red flower against a background of blue sky. Changing the way you see can be as simple as getting low or looking up.

How many great images have you missed because you forgot to look up? Get in the habit of looking up and you will be amazed at what you see. The light streaming through the roof of the Pantheon in Rome is unforgettable, but when captured on film it transforms the architecture into abstract modern shapes.

Reflections

Reflections are wonderful to look at and exciting to photograph because they can transform dull images into thrilling ones. Reflections show the mirror image of an object, creating harmony and often interesting abstractions. Beyond the exciting visual effects that reflections can bring to your photographs, it is just enormous fun to photograph them.

WATER REFLECTIONS Water is always changing with the light and the time of day. Sometimes the water is transparent, sometimes murky and at other times of day reflective—creating dancing bands of light. Use the reflections in water to echo the colors and patterns in a scene. Eliminate the object that is being reflected by placing only the reflection in the frame to create a mysterious and enigmatic photograph.

This tiny dancer was artfully captured by the photographer focusing on the image in the mirror instead of the mirror's surface. Photo: Paula DeReamer, Alexandria, Minnesota

MIRROR REFLECTIONS Getting remarkable photographs of reflections in a mirror looks deceptively simply but requires some degree of technical skill. To achieve proper focus, be sure to focus on the image in the mirror not the surface of the mirror. If you want yourself in the image you must be able to see yourself through the viewfinder. If you don't want yourself in the image, shoot from the side and not from the front. Whenever you can, avoid using your flash. The burst of light coming from your flash will bounce off the mirror and create a large hotspot that just might ruin the shot. Last, but not least, do not forget how to compose a great image. Get close, simplify a potentially cluttered and disorienting scene and choose a vertical or horizontal frame to match the subject.

Photographing water and reflective surfaces can fill your images with surprising visual dynamics.

TIP: A polarizing filter is ideal to use when photographing reflections or water because it reduces unwanted glare to give your images a cleaner look.

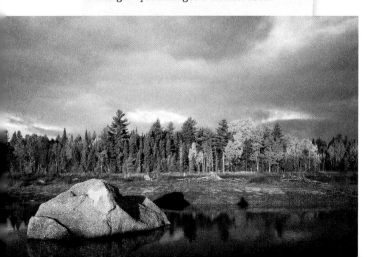

REFLECTIVE SURFACES City streets are an easy place to find reflections. Windows, like water, can reflect light or become completely transparent. If you look carefully you might even find some windows that, when photographed from a particular angle, will reflect the street and reveal the interior space at the same time. Try creating two portraits in one by photographing your best friend wearing dark sunglasses that reflect you taking the photograph. Be sure to get close enough so that you capture the detail. Modern architecture is perfect for finding reflective surfaces that can be composed into wonderful images. How about using reflective architectural surfaces to create a portrait? Place your subject in front of a reflective surface and move around until you get the most exciting image; photograph the reflection of the person rather than the actual person.

Dynamic Light

Fantastic visual effects can be found in lighting situations that many photographers purposely try to avoid. Extreme lighting conditions that contain areas within the scene that are very bright and very dark can cause images to become underexposed in the shadow areas or overexposed in the highlights. Avoiding these kinds of lighting situations is a missed opportunity to create dramatic images loaded with visual impact. With a little bit of practice and a brief technical review, you will soon be turning those challenging lighting situations into amazing visual opportunities that will transform your photographs.

SILHOUETTES A silhouette is an image that shows the solid black shape of an object against a bright background. Silhouette images captivate us because their stark black-and-white areas, with very little detail, create a two-dimensional effect. Backlit situations offer you the perfect opportunity to create silhouetted images. You can find backlit situations or you can create one by purposely moving your subject in front of a bright light source. Here are some simple steps for creating silhouettes with your camera:

One Identify that the scene has backlighting or create your own backlighting situation.

Two Take a light-meter reading by pointing your camera at the light. The recommended light-meter reading that you get for the scene will accommodate the bright light and create an exposure that will show detail in bright areas. Any object placed in front of that light will be underexposed and no detail will record on the film in these areas and the object will look black.

Three Adjust your camera to the recommended light-meter reading and take the shot.

Four To guarantee that you will get a silhouetted image, take a number of other exposures with different aperture/shutter combinations. By reducing the amount of light in the exposure, or underexposing, you will be sure to get an image that shows no detail in your main subject.

Silhouetted images are both a creative photographic technique and formal choice that reproduces an ethereal quality of light and graphic imagery. Silhouettes are wonderfully dramatic and very easy to make.

Skill builder

To technically conquer and creatively control extreme lighting situations, try this: Find a window in your home that looks out onto a brightly lit scene but does not have direct sunlight streaming in. Place an object, like flowers in a vase or an individual, directly in front of the window. Put your camera on a tripod, get a piece of paper and pencil and prepare to shoot at least 10 exposures of the scene. Start your note-taking with a light-meter reading to find out what recommended shutter speed and aperture combination is right for the scene and be sure to write that down. Keep careful notes about what aperture and shutter-speed combinations were used for each frame that you shoot. Use the recommended light-meter reading for your first shot. Then create a series of images adding more light than the recommended light-meter reading. If the light-meter reading was 1/500th at f/8, keep the camera set at f/8 and shoot six additional images changing the shutter speed to 1/250th, then 1/125, then 1/60th, then 1/30th, then 1/15th and finally 1/8th. This series of images will show you how adding more light than the recommended light-meter reading suggests will give you greater detail in the objects placed in front of the bright window. After that series is complete, create a second series that lets less light into the camera than the light-meter reading recommended. Starting with 1/500th at f/8, keep 1/500th as the shutter speed and begin closing down the aperture opening from f/8 to f/11 to f/16 and beyond if you have more aperture options. Letting less light into the camera will give you a series of images that shows how the background light is affected by exposure. Evaluate your film to learn how your light-meter adjustments affect exposure and how the visual dynamics of the image are enhanced by overriding your recommended light-meter reading.

Most photographers try to avoid shooting any subject that is positioned directly in front of a bright light because they do not want to create a silhouetted image. When exposed carefully, backlighting situations offer great opportunities to vary the look of your images and to capture incredible light in new ways.

DETAILED SUBJECT WITH A GLOWING BACKGROUND

If you want to use backlighting to create the kind of image that shows detail in the subject and wonderful glowing light in the background, you have to override your camera's recommended light-meter reading. Remember that the recommended reading will give you a silhouetted image. To avoid a silhouette you must increase the exposure so that detail will be captured in the foreground. Adjusting your exposure to get detail in the foreground will create an unusual image with ethereal qualities. It can turn the light into a halo of color surrounding your child's face or transform a canopy of flowering trees into a shimmering web. For backlit exposure with detail in the foreground, try these steps:

One Fill your camera's viewfinder with the foreground subject matter and adjust for a balanced exposure.

Two Back up and compose the photograph without changing your exposure settings and take the photograph.

GETTING DETAIL IN BOTH THE SUBJECT AND THE BRIGHT AREA

With a little help from an additional light source, it is possible to get detail in both the main subject and the bright area of a backlit subject. Remember that the contrast of the scene is so great that the film cannot handle this broad a spectrum of light. If you add light to the foreground then you are reducing the extreme contrast range. In a backlit situation fill flash is the perfect remedy. If the contrast between foreground and background is not too dramatic, placing a reflective surface—such as a white piece of foam core or mat board in the scene—can bounce enough light back at your subject to "even" the exposure. See pages 54-55 for detailed flash information.

BACKLIGHTING COMPENSATION

Many cameras have a backlighting-compensation feature that is very easy to use. You simply select the backlighting-compensation mode and point and shoot. In some cameras this feature automatically overexposes the image to prevent a silhouetted image from occurring. In other cameras the backlighting function will simply add flash to the exposure that illuminates the subject with light and balances out the contrast in the scene. If you have a backlighting feature, be sure to use it.

Scale

Inventive photographers use scale to create depth, establish the actual size that something is or to deliberately confuse the size that things should be. Scale is established by making comparisons between the size of things, like a ladybug and a leaf. Knowing how to create successful relationships of scale will help your photographs become more visually interesting and informative. Scale can transform the way you see a subject and add drama and a new layer of visual sophistication to your photographs.

CREATE DEEP SPACE Our understanding and interpretation of depth within a space is informed by the relationship of one object to another. When objects in the foreground are larger than objects in the background, a sense of deep space is created. In your images you can use this strategy to enhance and exaggerate the depth of space within a scene. By composing an image that places a large foreground object next to a small background object, you will establish a greater sense of depth within the space.

COMPARATIVE SCALE Our understanding of scale is informed by the relationship of one recognizable object to another. By purposely placing small objects next to big objects, you can reinforce how small something is or how big something is. A photograph of a very small dog sitting in the grass shows us what the dog looks like but does not tell us just how small he is. But a photograph of a very small dog sitting at the feet of an adult would show the viewer how small the dog actually is because it establishes a relationship of scale. How about photographing the bottom of your newborn's feet by having a big brother's feet in the photograph too? Your baby's foot will look small in comparison to big brother. Increase the sense of scale by adding Dad's feet to the photograph, too; now you have a photograph where baby's foot is tiny and brother's foot is small but Dad's foot is huge.

Using scale in your photographs to establish or confound our understanding of the size of things is a skill that takes very little time to master. The snowman in this image towers over my 8-month-old son and makes him look very small in comparison.

TRANSFORMING SCALE Knowing how to create and emphasize realistic scale relationships is the key to transforming the scale of things. By making small things in the foreground much bigger than the big things in the background, an exciting visual dynamic is created. If you ever visit the Leaning Tower of Pisa, you will see many photographers taking photos of people with their hands outstretched and the tower in the background. The resulting shot should look like the person is holding up the leaning tower. This photo cliché perfectly demonstrates how scale can be used in playful and transformative ways.

> **TIP:** Scale is established by making comparisons between objects within the scene. With a shallow depth of field, one object will be sharp while another object might be out of focus. With a long depth of field, all objects in the scene will be sharp. When all of the objects within the scene are sharp, establishing a particular sense of scale within the photograph will be more effective. Be sure to photograph with a small aperture opening so that the depth of field within the scene will be as long as it can be and all objects will be sharp.

Towering cypress trees create a visual tunnel that loom over the large Italian villa in the background. The effect of scale in this image implies deep space.

This photograph of the city being transported on the back of a flat bed truck is effective in transforming scale through the use of a long depth of field that gives both the foreground and middle ground great detail. It plays on our understanding that objects located in deep space will be less sharp than objects in the foreground.

Expert Advice: The Makings of a Visually Dynamic Photo
Angela Kelly, Associate Professor, Rochester Institute of Technology

THE MAKINGS OF A VISUALLY DYNAMIC PHOTO

Whether a photographic image is abstract or representational, black-and-white or color, it shares the fundamental principles of good design with other graphic media. The formal language of visual design can be read in terms of vantage point, scale, space, form and line, along with light and shadow. In many great photographs, the element of time creates visual impact. The larger meaning of images combines a strong visual language with the cultural and the symbolic. A photograph, which employs selective aspects of visual design well, transforms the familiar into the visually intriguing.

OBSERVING THE WORK OF OTHERS

Spend time looking at original work in galleries and museums. Observe the formal qualities mentioned above. Notice how an image describes the subject through framing, composition, lighting and color. Look to see if you can recognize the artist's visual signature style. When we experience a work of art, we sense it on a visceral level as well as on a cerebral one. Ask yourself, "How does the image make me feel?" and "Does it make me think?" Pay attention to how you arrive at those conclusions.

FINE-TUNING YOUR VISION

It is both challenging and rewarding to photograph a subject over time. In order to fine-tune your vision, shoot a lot more film than you think you will need. In this way you can experiment with different points of view, lenses, depth of field, apertures or shutter speed. Cover the subject from every angle and wait for the light to define the effect you want. Avoid gimmicks and clichés by training your eye to see and feel what is there, not just look for the obvious.

SHAKING THINGS UP

Rather than always viewing the visual world as static and ordered, try creating images in flux. A fun assignment is to create visually dynamic photographs by not looking through the viewfinder. Preset your camera to automatic for the correct exposure and take a series of photographs while moving and pointing your camera from different angles or vantage points. The images you get will be from an entirely different point of view from "normal."

ANGELA KELLY is an artist, educator and organizer. Originally from Belfast, North Ireland, she is currently an Associate Professor at RIT in Rochester, New York. Her work is included in collections worldwide, including The Center for Creative Photography in Tucson, The Art Institute of Chicago, The Mac Arthur Foundation, The Museum of Contemporary Photography in Chicago and The Arts Council of London. She has received grants and fellowships from The Arts Council of Great Britain and North Ireland, the National Endowment for the Arts, the Illinois Arts Council and The Focus Infinity Fund, as well as faculty development grants from RIT for her work. Her current digital work embodies an underlying narrative of loss, history and personal memory embedded in the Irish landscape and the Irish language. Working in and around the Irish coastal and interior areas of the "famine way," each image in the series represents a connection to a melancholic beauty, historical tragedy and to a language lost and found.

Mapping History/Mapping Identity. Iris Print on Somerset Velvet Watercolor Paper. 1998 © Angela Kelly. All rights reserved.

Photographing People

Photographing people is one of the greatest pleasures of being a photographer. The joy comes from spending time with people that you care about, sharing a laugh, a good cry or a once-in-a-lifetime moment.

When photographing strangers the camera often creates a situation where you get to make new friends, and often your subjects reveal something about themselves or their story that bonds you together. There is nothing more satisfying than seeing these special moments revealed in a remarkable portrait, one that truly captures the essence of the person you are photographing.

This chapter will help you make better portraits by showing you terrific examples of successful images and giving you the practical information you need to create expressive portraits. You will learn the unique approaches used by professional portrait photographers to place your subject at ease and create a photograph with meaning. Making an excellent portrait is an exciting and rewarding challenge. Enjoy every moment of it!

Luca

FISH

Luca had always taken to water like a fish, and as soon as he learned to swim well enough to go into the pool's deep end, he was bold enough to jump off the diving board. Our little daredevil showed no hesitation whatsoever!

Luca, age 5

Great Portraits

Amazing portraits happen when everything comes together in just the right way. It is like making a cake: You start with a list of ingredients, mix them all together, put it in the oven to bake and enjoy how others appreciate it. What separates a good cake from an incredible cake is the cook and his or her intuitive understanding of the ingredients, inventive experimentation and desire to make it great. The essential ingredients of a portrait are good camera skills, creative use of camera functions, dynamic visual impact, expressive lighting, an enthusiastic photographer, a willing subject and practice. What makes a great portrait awesome is the ability of the photographer to put all of these ingredients together in inventive ways and the photographer's ability to inspire the subject into revealing his or her soul.

Successful portraits depend upon willing subjects. This couple was very comfortable being photographed and allowed me to work with them for over an hour. Direct eye contact and body language is an important ingredient in fabulous portraits.

EQUIPMENT Knowing how your camera works and having confidence in using it will help you to focus all of your energy on the person you are photographing instead of on your equipment. Remember to consider the lighting situation, slower ISO film (50, 64, 100 speed) for shooting outdoors or faster ISO film (200 or 400 speed) for shooting in low light. If you are shooting with a digital camera, select the resolution and file format that will give you the best results for what you have in mind. Most photographers prefer to use an 85mm to 105mm lens for portraiture because of the way it compresses space and is more flattering than wide-angle lenses. If you have a tripod and cable release, be sure to bring them. Shooting a portrait with your camera on a tripod will help you create a more relaxed and conversational atmosphere during the shoot. If you simply stand behind your camera and tripod, once you have your subject framed and in focus, you can talk to your subject without having your face hidden behind the camera. This technique allows your subject to forget about the portrait session and be more spontaneous. Don't forget extra batteries. Before any photo shoot, make sure that you have everything you need and that your camera is in good working order.

CREATIVE CAMERA CONTROLS Some portraits look just wonderful when the background is a wash of color while other portraits are terrific with focused detail throughout the entire frame. Remember that large aperture openings like f/2, f/3.5, f/4 and f/5.6 will give you a shallow depth of field or a narrow range of focus. Small aperture openings such as f/22, f/16 and f/11 will give you a long depth of field or a broader range of focus. Choose the depth of field that is right for both the subject and the scene you are photographing. If the background is cluttered and not very interesting, use a shallow depth of field to take the emphasis off the background and keep it on your subject. If the background is wonderful and you want to use it to add information to the subject, choose a long depth of field so that as much of the scene as possible is in sharp focus. Depth of field is a visual element that can add emotion to the image. A shallow depth of field creates a soft, romantic atmosphere. A long depth of field can be used to create a masculine and direct impression.

When considering the shutter speed, remember to reduce image blur caused by hand-holding your camera. An easy rule to remember is to use a tripod when your shutter speed is slower than the focal length of your lens. For example, if you are using a 105mm lens you would want to use a shutter speed of 1/125th of a second or faster as the next slower shutter speed is 1/60th of a second. The use of movement in the image if intentional can be used to your advantage. Movement can add wonderful qualities to a portrait. With a thoughtful choice of shutter speed, you can slow down movement, creating a blurring ethereal presence in the image, or you can stop the action with a fast shutter speed creating visual tension. Both can be powerful; let your subject determine the look you want.

Light is a key ingredient to successful portrait images. The quality of light establishes mood, influences color and enhances the physical attributes of your subject. Photo: Andrea Zocchi © All rights reserved.

VISUAL DYNAMICS When photographing people, many photographers forget about visual dynamics. While the photographer may have captured a great expression, the image as a whole may not be very interesting. In portraiture visual dynamics are important. They can be used to add symbolic elements and psychological qualities to the image that serve to emphasize the personality of the individual being photographed. Everything about the composition should reinforce the character of the individual you are photographing. A composition that fills the frame with visual complexity and places the subject off-center evokes a complex character. A simple background with a centered subject implies straightforward openness. Consider your point of view. If you want the person to look heroic, get your camera low and shoot looking up. If you want the person to look small, get up high and shoot down. Backlighting and silhouettes offer clever opportunities to enhance certain personality traits. Scale can be used to create relationships of size and to underscore contrasting qualities in an individual.

TIP: Get in the habit of checking and reorganizing your camera equipment after a shoot. If you always put your equipment back in the bag in the same place, you will never have to miss a shot because you had to fish around in your bag for your favorite lens. You will know exactly where it is and after a while you won't even have to look in your bag to get it. After the shoot check your camera battery and make sure that you have an extra camera battery in your bag. Clean your lenses with a lens-cleaning cloth and put them back in their cases or bags if you have them. Reorganize and store any other pieces of equipment that you might have used. Then put your camera bag in an easy-to-grab spot for the next time you go out to shoot.

LOCATION Too often a good portrait is ruined because the photographer didn't take the extra step to move the subject just one foot to the right or left. The location that you choose to create the portrait in can add visual complexity and dynamic elements like curves or angles to your composition. Location can be used to establish the significance of an event, such as a graduation or wedding. Scale in the location can be used to create relationships of size and to underscore contrasting qualities in an individual. Choosing a location with a simple background focuses the viewer's attention directly on the individual being photographed. Always remember before making your portrait to look around you; the best background could be just off to your right or left.

Environmental portraits show an individual in relationship to their surroundings. These kinds of portraits are terrific to make when you are traveling or photographing special events.

Take advantage of graphic visual elements in the scene that can be used to accentuate the portrait and separate the individual from the background. Photo: Andrea Zocchi © All rights reserved.

LIGHTING The purposeful use of lighting is a good way to add a professional look to your portraiture and to enhance the emotional characteristics you are trying to accentuate. The very language used to describe the qualities of light also describes the psychological effect of light—soft and hard, warm and cool, natural and artificial, direct and reflected. Control the light by choosing a particular time of day to shoot. Check the weather forecast and plan to shoot on the day that suits the image. Rain, snow, impending storm, bright sun, puffy clouds—all of these weather situations offer unique creative possibilities of light. Looking for dramatic light? To create an angelic effect, use backlighting to fill the photograph with light and to create a halo around the subject. A silhouetted image can add power and strength to the photograph. How about shooting by candlelight or flashlight? Shadows can be fantastic physical and psychological elements in a photograph. A shuttered window with streaming light can paint black-and-white stripes across the subject. Flash as the main light source in a darkened environment will create intense contrast. Use fill flash to open up the shadow areas and to even out contrasty light. Mix light sources like flash and tungsten, causing vibrant and unusual color combinations on film. Once you get the hang of controlling light, you will be amazed at the technical and creative leaps and bounds that your portrait photographs will take.

The Subject

Capturing the essence of the individual you are photographing is the biggest challenge in portraiture. Photographs that reveal the personality of the subjects are exciting, engaging and always unique. Taking your portrait photographs beyond a purely descriptive image is easy to do. You can make immense improvements to your portraits by simply paying more attention to your subject. The key elements to consider are the unique personality traits of the individual you are photographing, his or her facial expressions, body language or pose and the clothing he or she is wearing for the shoot.

Clothing tells a lot about a person because it gives us clues to the individual's personality. Clothing can indicate if the person is playful or serious, formal or informal and confident or self-conscious. It can describe what the person does for a living, what his or her hobbies are or what country he or she is from. If you have an opportunity to request particular clothing for the shoot, take advantage of it.

Once you begin shooting, pay close attention to the facial expression, body language and pose of your subject. The facial expression sets the tone of the image. Look for expressive moments that capture the personality traits that you hope to reveal in the photograph. Notice the body language of the subject. Arms folded across the chest imply a closed personality. Hands placed on the hips suggest defiance. An open palm could suggest vulnerability while tightly clasped hands imply tension. Hands propping up a chin or held to the side a face can imply confidence. Almost all subjects want to know what to do with their hands, so simply tell them what you want. This kind of question is an open invitation for you to make the image that you envision.

Every human being has unique qualities and characteristics that define his or her personality. Capturing these qualities on film requires thoughtful consideration of clothing, facial expression, body language, visual dynamics and the location that you choose to photograph individuals in. The image of a cowboy reveals a casual and playful personality while the black-and-white image shows a formal and serious personality.

Skill builder

Before you shoot make a list of the qualities of the individual you are going to photograph. If I were to make this list for my son Luca, I would write: always moving, kindhearted, impatient, athletic, stubborn, outgoing, thoughtful about others, likes to tell jokes, compassionate and sweet. For my son Marco, the list would look like this: funny, determined, sensitive, introverted, moody, intensely focused or completely disorganized (one or the other) and loves helping those who need help. Once you have created the list, consider which qualities you would like to bring out in the photograph. Then take those personality traits and write down ways that you can visually bring those qualities to life in the image. Use the categories of creative camera controls, visual dynamics and lighting to help you brainstorm ideas.

The Photographer

Every portrait photograph made is a collaboration between the photographer and the person or people being photographed. The success of the image is directly related to the success of the collaboration. Successful collaborations require honesty and trust, a positive attitude, compromises, sincerity and patience. There are many things that a photographer can do to make the collaboration go smoothly.

Getting permission to photograph is the first step in the collaboration. With children permission is a must but remember that you cannot simply ask the child for permission, you need to ask a parent. Tell the person that you want to photograph him or her and why you want to photograph the person. Telling them why you want to photograph him or her will let the person know what your intentions are. Tell the person what you find interesting about him or her and what aspects of his or her personality you are hoping to capture. When the subject knows what you want in the photograph, you will be more likely to get it.

How the photographer approaches the subject and works with individuals can determine how successful the photograph will be. Making great portraits requires the photographer to be sensitive, flexible and inventive. Photographing children requires the photographer to behave and interact very differently than when photographing adults.

TIP: Sometimes the key to making a great portrait is an opportunity to photograph the same person a second time. After you have seen the images from the first shoot and have had a chance to think about what was great and what needs improvement, you might ask to meet that person again. This time you can show the subject what you got and what you didn't get. You can talk with the person about ways to improve the photographs by getting his or her input and sharing your ideas. Shooting an individual for the second, third or even fourth time can be helpful in getting closer and closer to a portrait that captures the true personality of the individual.

Be positive and energetic during the shoot. Ask your subject if he or she has any suggestions about how to capture the characteristics you are hoping to capture. Get a conversation going with your subject; it will help you get to know him or her better and it might inspire interesting expressions. Help your subject feel comfortable in front of the camera. I often invite people to have a look at what I am seeing. I will put myself in the scene where the subject was and ask him or her to look through the camera to get an idea of what the image will look like. Those of you with digital cameras have a significant advantage in this regard because you can simply show the subject the photographs you are making. Be sensitive about when the subject has had enough and is ready to stop. Stopping the shoot at the right time is an important consideration. If you leave your subject feeling that it was just too much, you will not be able to photograph the person again.

There are some people who like to be photographed and some people that simply hate it. In my experience, the people who like to be photographed have a lot of self-confidence and enjoy the attention. People who don't like to be photographed often feel that they look terrible in photographs and they don't like the feeling of being observed so closely by the photographer. The challenge of photographing individuals who like to be photographed is that they often take over the shoot. They set the pose and they give you their biggest "cheese" smile and then wait for you to take the photograph. While their willingness to be photographed is extremely important to the success of the image, it can also be a drawback because the resulting photographs are often predictable and do not truly capture the unique qualities of the individual being photographed. In these situations the photographer really needs to take control of the shoot in a positive way. With enthusiastic individuals it helps to make a number of photographs exactly the way that they want, then take your turn to get the photographs that you want.

For subjects who are uncomfortable in front of the camera, the photographer needs to create an upbeat and positive atmosphere during the shoot. These individuals often like to be told exactly what to do, so be sure to give them plenty of direction. Start shooting from a distance and as the subject begins to feel more comfortable you can begin to get closer. Be sure to continue telling your subject what is great about how he or she looks in front of the camera as you shoot. With some individuals it helps to take their mind off of being photographed. Find out what their interests are and get them talking about the things that they really care about.

Casual vs. Formal Portraits

Most people assume that a candid portrait is a photograph taken without the subject aware of the fact that he or she is being photographed. We make this assumption because candid portraits typically do not show eye contact between the subject and the camera. The subject is usually engaged in an activity and is photographed in a relaxed or natural pose. Many exceptional "candid" portraits are taken with the subject well aware of being photographed and the pose often directed by the photographer. To use the word "candid" is to imply a snapshot or a photograph taken rather than made. I prefer to use the word casual to describe and define a portrait that reveals a more natural pose, shows an individual engaged in an activity or captures an individual that is not making eye contact with the camera. Formal portraits are photographs that are obviously directed by the photographer. In a formal portrait the subject is looking into the camera and the pose is purposeful. The choice to shoot a casual or formal portrait should be dictated by your subject. If your subject has an informal and open personality then a casual shot will echo that personality. If your subject's personality is all business—or serious and direct—a formal portrait would help to accent those traits.

PROPS FOR ADULTS
Many individuals feel more comfortable being photographed with something in their hands or something in the scene to lean against. Props can also give insight into the person you are photographing. If your brother-in-law just finished restoring his 1965 Mustang, photograph him in it or leaning up against it. If your sister loves to garden, have her hold her favorite flowers or vegetables. If your father plays the piano, photograph him with his hands resting on the keys. Having a prop in the scene also serves as a great starting point for conversations that will lead to a more relaxed atmosphere for the shoot.

TAKE THE TIME YOU NEED
Photographing adults offers a unique opportunity to experiment with the image. Most adults are happy to work with the photographer to get just the right shot. When photographing an adult, arrange to photograph for a certain amount of time. I believe that 45 minutes to an hour is just about right. To make a fantastic portrait, you need time to get yourself visually warmed up, to get your subject comfortable and to get into the groove of shooting.

PAY ATTENTION TO YOUR GUT INSTINCT
When you are shooting and all of a sudden you get this feeling that the photograph you are making is going to be an awesome one, take a few moments to make several variations of that idea. Ask the subject to hold that pose as you try a number of slightly different camera angles or aperture settings. Or you might need to stay right where you are and ask the subject to tilt his or her head slightly or to change the position of his or her hands. You never know; the third, fourth or fifth version of that one great shot may make the shot even better. Sometimes the slightest variation is the key to an amazing image.

To create this portrait of my best friend, I brought along a book for her to hold. She had just gone back to school to finish her degree so the book is significant in the image and it helped make a more natural-looking expression because she felt comfortable holding the familiar object in her hands for the photograph.

Skill builder
To build your confidence and skill in creating quality portraits, practice with individuals whom you are very comfortable with. Ask a friend or your spouse to work with you so that you can build your portrait skills. I recommend that you photograph an adult rather than a child because an adult will be able to give you the time that you need to photograph and can collaborate with you more thoughtfully. Shoot an entire roll of film of one individual. Experiment with the ways in which you direct the subject to pose. Explore ways to inspire a variety of facial expressions in your subject. Practice capturing directed images and undirected moments. As you become more comfortable creating portraits of those you know well, move on to photographing individuals that you do not know as well. Offering to give your subject a copy of one of the images is a fun way to thank the individual for agreeing to be photographed.

To get this photograph I was standing in water up to my knees but I just couldn't resist the quality of light and my son's pure joy at being in the water. Shooting the image horizontally centered him in the vast expanse of the water. To energize the composition I asked him to spread his arms out across the water. It made him smile and helped to create a more visually dynamic image.

Photographing Children

Without a doubt, children are both the easiest and most difficult subjects to photograph. All children are amazing individuals who are full of expression, energy and imagination. The key to a successful shoot with children is the mood of the child. A happy, cooperative child is a pleasure to photograph. A grumpy child ends the photo shoot quickly. There are many things that a photographer can do to help make photographing a child both fun and productive.

It's amazing how clothing can influence the pose and expressions of children. Dressed in a black velvet dress, this little girl strikes a formal pose and a serious look. When dressed casually in a T-shirt, she instinctively assumes a playful expression and pose. When photographing children, consider whether or not you want to create a more serious formal portrait or a casual playful portrait. Dressing children accordingly will help you get the results you are looking for. Photos: Ellen Hargrove, Jenks, Oklahoma

GO WITH THE FLOW
As those of you with children know, it takes patience to work with kids. They have short attention spans and are easily distracted. When you have a child's undivided attention, take advantage of it but don't overdo it. You will keep kids happier longer and get considerable results when you photograph in short bursts of time and give kids an opportunity to play in between. It is also a good idea to shoot a lot of film with children. Kids close their eyes, look away and fidget just when you are taking the shot.

CAPTURING EXPRESSIVE EXPRESSIONS
Too often kids are photographed from the standing height of the photographer. Kids will respond a lot better when the photographer gets down to their level. When you are face to face with a child, he or she will be less intimidated and shy. And for those kids who are not shy at all, getting down low will help you get their attention. If you can, set your tripod up and get out from behind the camera. With children, eye contact is everything and the minute you put your head behind the camera, eye contact is lost and they think you have moved on to something else—so they do too. If you are expressive, a child will be expressive. Laugh with them, make silly faces right back and if you want a serious portrait, show them what you mean then have fun with them practicing it. Don't ask kids to smile because it always looks forced. Give them something to smile about and the expression will be genuine.

This photograph of Julia was taken after she and I talked for a long while about what kind of queen she was, what kind of castle she lived in and what kind of knights she had in her court. Our conversation broke the ice and led to a natural and compelling portrait photograph.

GET HELP

Photographing children is much easier when you have help. Most children do much better when they are entertained or paid attention to. A willing assistant can help you make children laugh, keep them sitting in the same place, have the snacks ready to go or throw a ball with them while you are changing film. By having an assistant you will be able to focus more of your energy on the creation of the photograph. Moms, dads, grandparents, brothers or sisters could all be assistants. The key to a helpful assistant is your ability to tell the assistant exactly what you want him or her to do and what kind of photograph you are hoping to take. If you are working alone, remember that kids love to help. If you let the child that you are photographing help you in any way, he or she will become more invested in making a good photograph. Let the child set the tripod up or help you do it. Ask him or her to take the lid off the film canister because the child is much stronger than you are. Or ask a child to move the chair over into the light. Kids really do love to help so let them help as much as you can. Another way to get help is to bring along a puppet. Give the puppet a name and tell the child that the silly parrot in your hand, named Polly of course, is your assistant. The child will get such a kick out of it and just might respond better to the parrot telling him or her what to do than the photographer.

KIDS LOVE PROPS

With a little imagination you can find a world of fun props that can be used to help make terrific photographs of kids. Excellent props for kids include bubbles, hats, puppets, angel wings, baskets to sit in, colorful umbrellas, tire swings, a tea set, stuffed animals, kites, riding toys, butterfly nets, a child-sized rocking chair and countless other items. Using interesting props when photographing kids can serve two very important purposes. Great props will give you opportunities to add visual dynamics to your images with added color and shapes. Children just love props and will interact with any object you give them. Their interactions with props will create more varied expressions to photograph and help keep those little attention spans activated for longer amounts of time as you photograph. Be sure that the props you give to children are age-appropriate and safe.

CATCHING MOVEMENT

Since kids are always moving, don't try to fight it. Instead, try capturing their energy on film. Use a slow shutter speed and let them move. The slower the shutter speed, the blurrier they will be. Make sure you experiment with a number of different shutter speeds to get the results you are after. With a slow shutter speed on a stable camera, the child will appear in motion. Instead of blurring the child try blurring the background. Use a slow shutter speed and get on the merry-go-round or seesaw with him or her. As the camera moves with the subject, the child will be in sharp focus and the background will be blurred. Again don't forget to try a variety of shutter speeds to capture just the right amount of movement.

Direct eye contact in a portrait engages the viewer to look closer at the image, but getting children to look into the camera is no easy task. When looking for eye contact, photographers should be prepared to shoot many images and to tell a lot of funny jokes and make silly noises to get a child's attention.

TIP: Before photographing children, prepare a few props for the scene. If you are working outdoors, have a few props ready to go, such as sidewalk chalk, gardening gloves and a planter full of flowers or beach ball and colorful beach towel. If you are working indoors, collect a few props for the photograph, like a cozy blanket placed on an overstuffed chair, favorite costumes or drawing supplies.

Photographing Babies

Photographing babies is another ball game altogether because the strategies that photographers normally use to create portraits simply do not apply. Babies fall asleep at the drop of a hat, they drool and spit up, they laugh, they cry and coo to communicate and they cannot hold a pose. They are a wonderful challenge to photograph and will require as much imagination as you can muster. Making wonderful photographs of babies that melt hearts is within your reach.

SAFETY CONSIDERATIONS The primary concern when photographing babies is safety. A baby should never be propped up in or on something that he or she could fall out of. Always work at ground level so that babies cannot fall from any height. Surround the baby with pillows just in case. Babies can never be left alone at any time. Do not give a baby any prop or toy that is not age-appropriate. Never cover a baby's face with anything or place anything in the scene that the baby could grab and harm himself with. Safety is your number-one concern.

POSING BABIES The four basic poses to consider when photographing young babies are lying on their backs, on their tummies, sitting up or held in someone's arms. When photographing a baby lying flat on her back or tummy, get directly above her and shoot straight down or lie right down next to her and photograph from eye level. Consider your distance from the baby. If you are up high looking down, the baby will seem small compared to all that is around her. Try photographing the baby so her entire body fills the frame of the image. Then get really close and fill the frame with the baby's face. A great way to vary the angles and poses that you can use in photographing babies is to ask the parents to give you a hand. Think about how one or both parents can be used as a backdrop in the portrait. Photograph a close-up of the baby cradled in Dad's arms. Place the baby on Mom's chest and have them lie down together. Have Mom and Dad intertwine their arms together and place the baby in their arms. Beyond tummies and backs, larger babies who can sit up on their own can be photographed in a greater variety of poses. The most important thing to consider with a sitting pose is shooting from eye level.

There are a limited number of poses that can be used when photographing young babies. These limitations require photographers to carefully consider all of the other visual aspects of the image that can be used to energize the portrait. The visual elements of color, light, texture, background, point of view, expression and composition become even more important when photographing babies.

Constructing exciting portraits of a baby can be as simple as paying attention to color schemes. The American flag in this image creates a bold and exciting pattern that matches the expression and pose of this baby. The red shirt and blue overalls that the baby is wearing echo the colors in the flag and add an element of patriotism. Photo: Sandy Puc © All rights reserved.

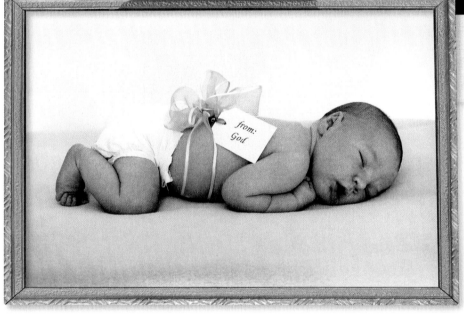

TIP: Placing a baby on a beanbag chair covered in some terrific fabric can be a great way to adjust the postition and poses of babies.

Constructing scenes and adding props to the image can help to make wonderful portraits of babies. Successfully constructed images are carefully planned and photographed to reveal specific visual and emotional qualities. Photo: Molly Sheedlo, Blaine, Minnesota

CONSTRUCTING THE SWEETEST BABY PORTRAITS

Given the limitation of the poses that can be used with babies, many baby photographs look alike. A clever way to make your baby portraits stand out is to construct a wonderful scene for the photograph. For babies who are lying on their backs or stomachs, consider what they are lying on. A yard of wonderful fabric like satin or white lace placed over red velvet would make a wonderful background and add visual interest to the photograph. How about placing silk flowers around the baby to create a frame-within-a-frame? Get a big basket that the baby could fit comfortably in. Put a pillow in the basket and cover the pillow with a handmade baby blanket. Then weave flowers through the top of the basket to make a beautiful border. If you are photographing a baby with a parent, consider what the backdrop looks like. If the baby is naked, perhaps the parent should be too. Or try covering the mom in lace and letting the baby rest in her arms. Consider constructing an entire scene for larger babies who can sit. Remember constructions can be both indoors and outdoors. Start with a chair or a place for the baby to sit and work around it. If you can get your hands on a child's rocking chair, a small beanbag chair, a tiny bench or even a rocking horse—that would be great. Adult-size chairs can be interesting and useful backdrops. Then consider the background. Draping fabric behind the chair can add interesting color or texture. Add elements to the scene such as flowerpots, a kite, an umbrella or baskets.

Photographing Teenagers

Teenagers are complex individuals who require thoughtful consideration when being photographed. They want to be treated like adults, and they demand our respect. They can be refreshingly funny and intensely serious at any given time. They are passionate about their hobbies, their friends and the issues that they care about. A teenager's multifaceted qualities offer endless potential for exciting and refreshingly unpredictable portraits.

TEENSPEAK: TELL IT LIKE IT IS

Teenagers are wired to detect sincerity, so it is very important to tell it like it is. Tell them why you want to photograph them and how long you think it might take. As you are shooting, be sure to tell them how excited you are about what you are seeing in the photograph and let them know exactly what that is. Give them some control in making the photographs and your shoot will be more successful. Ask them to get into their favorite clothes and to bring their most precious possession for the photograph. Ask them if they would like to help you create a background for the photograph. During the shoot put the camera in their hands and let them photograph you just for the fun of it.

TIP: Consider creating a series of portraits that you can frame together in a grid or a line. Photograph your teen in serious and playful moments, dressed up or in a pair of jeans and T-shirt, close-ups or full-body shots. A variety of images will help to show the many facets of his or her personality.

CAPTURE THE TEEN'S PASSION

Teenagers are active beings and passionate about their interests. Creating a portrait that shows that passion is a clever way to photograph a teen. If they love sports, make a photograph of them in uniform holding their sport ball or a piece of related sports equipment. If they play music, photograph them with their instrument. If they love chess, make a portrait of them with a chessboard. Energize the portrait by creating an active pose. Get them playing their instrument or throwing the ball and catching it. When you see a moment that is exciting, ask them to hold the pose or repeat the action so that you can take it again. Be sure to ask them about what they love to do and why. Ask them how they got started and what their all-time favorite moment was. Asking them direct questions will bring out their excitement in the photograph. A teenager's life is often so hectic, but setting aside time to photograph is a wonderful way to learn something new about him or her and to stay in tune with what your teen is up to.

LET TEENS BE WHO THEY ARE

Natural poses work best with teens. Teens can be easily embarrassed and are often self-conscious. Let them take the lead with the expressions and poses that they feel comfortable with. After they warm up to the camera and begin to relax, work out of that first pose and into others. As you begin to work into other poses remember to stay away from forced expressions and unnatural poses. Individuals who feel uncomfortable in front of the camera will look uncomfortable in the final image, so be sensitive to how they feel.

When photographing teenagers, pay close attention to their comfort level so that you can capture personality and expression. If you photograph teens with props that are connected to their passions or hobbies you will be able to capture more natural and comfortable expressions.

Photographing Groups

Group portraits are wonderful opportunities to create lasting images of friends and loved ones. With thoughtful consideration about what group shots can be and deliberate choices about how individuals relate to each other in the image, how they are arranged in the frame, the location for the shot and how your subjects are dressed will transform your photographs from snapshots into portraits that will stand the test of time.

These best friends have a very close relationship that is revealed in the tilt of their heads, physical proximity and facial expressions.

CREATING LASTING IMAGES

Most of us approach making a group portrait as a simple visual record of what individuals look like, but group portraits can be so much more than that. Group portraits can illuminate the physical and emotional relationships between individuals. Group portraits can show how we care about each other and the bonds that exist between us. The first step toward making wonderful group portraits is to change your expectations of what a group portrait can be. Go beyond the surface by photographing to capture the unique qualities of the relationship between the individuals you are photographing. Start by making a list of the qualities that describe the relationship between the individuals you are going to photograph. Then ask your subjects to tell you what they think those qualities are. As you photograph, look for ways to bring those qualities into the photograph.

To create a visually dynamic group portrait often requires simplifying the image. In this photograph the subjects were asked to wear all black for the shoot. A black backdrop was placed behind the group and the photographer moved in close enough to capture all four faces. The photographer also directed the parents to look down while the children looked right into the camera. The final image was printed in black-and-white further accentuating the visual dynamics of the image. Photo: Sandy Puc © All rights reserved.

HOW INDIVIDUALS RELATE TO EACH OTHER WITHIN A GROUP

The physical contact portrayed between individuals is the most significant clue to the nature of a relationship. A baby cradled in someone's arms shows nurturing. Two sisters with arms wrapped around each other in a gentle hug show love. A woman's head resting on her husband's shoulder shows intimacy. Two best friends sitting back-to-back show individuality and the bonds of friendship at the same time. To add more emotional depth to your photographs, direct your subjects into poses that show physical contact between individuals.

CONSTRUCTING DYNAMIC GROUP ARRANGEMENTS

A careful arrangement of the individuals in a group shot can add terrific visual dynamics to the photograph. Arrange individuals within the scene to create simple shapes. A triangle shape can be created when placing taller individuals in the back with smaller people standing in front. Arrange your group in a circle by having taller people standing in the back, medium-height people standing on the sides and the smallest standing in the middle in front of everyone else. If you then ask them all to put one hand on a neighbor's shoulder, the effect of the circle will be even more pronounced.

SIMPLIFY THE BACKGROUND IN GROUP SHOTS

To create visually effective group portraits, the photographer must consider how the background of the scene looks in the image. Visually complicated backgrounds and locations should be avoided with group portraiture because photographing with more than one person in the image is already visually complex. Simple backgrounds will help to focus the viewer's attention on the subjects in the photograph. Create simplified backgrounds by carefully choosing the location you are shooting in and paying close attention to your depth of field.

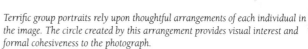

Terrific group portraits rely upon thoughtful arrangements of each individual in the image. The circle created by this arrangement provides visual interest and formal cohesiveness to the photograph.

CLOTHING FOR GROUP PHOTOS

It is very difficult to get visual unity in a group portrait when one person is dressed in a suit, another in shorts and a T-shirt, another in bright red and yet another in a blue-green plaid. Take some control over the way your subjects are dressed, and your photographs will look cohesive. Determine if the photograph will be casual or formal and decide upon a color scheme of one or two colors. For a casual look, jeans and white shirts would do.

For a more formal look, how about everyone in black? Choose solid colors to keep the image simple. Take it a step further and consider how the background colors work with the clothing in the group. Create harmony throughout the entire photograph by choosing a simple background that contains a color from within the color scheme you have determined to use.

Skill builder

Two essential elements of creating a successful group portrait are the ability of the photographer to direct the photograph and creating interesting arrangements of the individuals being photographed. To build your skills in these areas, recruit a group of three or more individuals that would be willing to work with you for a shoot. Before shooting, imagine as many different locations and arrangements who you can think of. When you have the group assembled, direct the group into the arrangements that you thought of ahead of time. Pay close attention to how you are directing the subjects, your tone, your enthusiasm and the ways in which you describe what you want them to do. After you have shot all the images that you had in mind, begin venturing into unknown territory. Make things up as you go along to see where they might lead you. When you practice a variety of arrangements and how to work with a group, then you will be better prepared to make terrific group shots when those opportunities arise.

Creating a Home Studio

Setting up a home studio is easy to do and worthwhile as it will give your photographs a unique, professional look. All you need is a space to work in, light and a few pieces of inexpensive equipment and you will be off and running. Creating a home studio is an inexpensive way to transform the way your photographs look.

SPACE CONSIDERATIONS FOR A HOME STUDIO
The ideal space for a shooting studio would be a space large enough for you to create a backdrop in, to set up props and allow you to step far enough away from the subject to capture the entire individual in the frame. Studio spaces can be a corner of a room, a garage, an extra bedroom or a porch. Depending upon the use of the space, you can easily set up either a temporary or permanent shooting studio.

ATTENTION ON LIGHT IN A HOME STUDIO
The quality of light is an important consideration when finding the right space to transform into a studio. You will want to choose a space that has natural light. Large windows or doors that can be opened are a must. Natural light is the most beautiful light source and the more you have of it, the better the images will look. Remember that you need enough light to create a good exposure. Be careful about direct light streaming through a window in the afternoon or early morning. Contrasty light creates harsh shadows that are difficult to control visually and to expose accurately. Soft light is ideal and north-facing windows are the best. Remember that early morning and afternoon light is warmer in color than midday light. With natural light as the light source, you can shoot color film balanced for daylight and not have to worry about color shifts caused by film and artificial light combinations.

Find a space with good light, such as an airy garage, and clear it out.

Hang a backdrop in your studio and position your subject in front of it. If your subject is too close to the backdrop, you will see shadows and imperfections or wrinkles in the backdrop on the photograph.

If you do not have a space that has natural light, then consider getting some clamp lights or photolamps to supplement other lights in the space. Clamp lights and photolamps use tungsten bulbs, so remember that if you are going to shoot color film you will need to use color film balanced for tungsten light. Rather exciting color combinations can be achieved by mixing both natural and artificial light together. You could use natural light as the main light source then shine a clamp light into the scene to light up a side of the subject's face with a touch of yellow-orange.

Avoid exposure problems caused by backlighting. If there are any windows in the space, you will want to photograph with the windows to the side of the subject or behind the photographer. If you are looking for more dramatic possibilities, position your subject directly in front of the window and create a silhouetted image or backlit halo around the portrait. Don't forget about using your flash as fill or as the primary light source option for your home studio.

You can further control the lighting by purchasing or making a reflector that will bounce the light into specific areas of the image. With some lighting situations, unwanted shadows can obscure details that you might want to capture in the scene. Light coming in from a window that is positioned on the left side of your subject's face could cause a deep shadow on the right. If you have a reflector you can bounce the light coming in from the window off of a reflector and onto the shadowed side of your subject to illuminate your subject beautifully. To make a reflector, cover a large piece of cardboard in aluminum foil or white paper. Or use a large sheet of white foam core board. Make a variety of reflectors in different sizes that you can use as you need to. Holding the reflector while you photograph is a juggling act, so purchase an extra light stand that you can clamp the reflector to during the shoot. Try shifting the angle of the reflector to modify the light. The closer the reflector is to the subject, the brighter the bounced-light effect will be.

> **TIP:** A lighting strategy in filmmaking is to light a subject with both warm and cool light. You can add color to your reflector by covering it in cloth. Choose a bright, warm color and be sure that the cloth is reflective. Shiny nylon is a great choice. The shiny cloth will reflect that color into the scene.

Position yourself a few feet from the subject and begin photographing.

Controlling the light and removing unwanted backgrounds or creating great backdrops leads to successful images. Photos: Kelli Noto, Centennial, Colorado

Home studio equipment

Lights and backdrops are the essential pieces of equipment you will need for your studio. Clamp lights that you can purchase at any hardware store are an inexpensive and useful piece of equipment to have. Purchase some simple light stands that will allow you to set up your clamp lights wherever you need them to be and to easily move them around the space as you need to. Let your imagination run wild about the backdrops you use in the scene. Fabric backdrops are easy to use and easy to get your hands on. Visit your local hobby or fabric store and browse the remnant and sale sections for great buys and interesting materials. Scout kitchen and bath

stores for tablecloths or bedsheets. Consider inventing your own backdrops. Draw on rolls of paper that you can hang in the scene. I once used large sheets of bubble wrap as a backdrop. How about taking a few large sheets of poster board and gluing colorful fall leaves onto it? To hang the backdrop, take an old broom handle and clamp the backdrop to it. Then simply hang or design uprights that will support the broom handle with the backdrop hanging off of it. To store your backdrops roll them up onto the broom handle and put them in a safe place for your next portrait shoot.

Taking Your Studio on the Road

Small things can make a big difference. You can change the look of your images from amateur to professional by taking your studio on the road. Traveling with your lighting studio will give you more opportunities to create wonderful lighting for your photographs and to have creative control over the visual dynamics in your images.

LIGHTS Creating a portable studio for both indoor and outdoor use will give you the greatest flexibility to respond to any situation that you might find yourself photographing in. If you know that you will have access to electricity, then you can bring a set of lights. With your clamp lights you will want to carry light stands or be sure that there are objects nearby that you can clamp the lights onto. Light stands will give you the greatest flexibility for placing your lights where you want them to be. Be sure to carry extra bulbs and an extension cord. Duct tape is good to have in your bag in case you need to tape down light cords on the floor for safety and to avoid the lights falling over because someone tripped over the cord. Large duffle bags are an excellent way to get all your studio gear into one bag.

REFLECTORS When photographing outdoors the light is almost always beautiful. Modifying this natural beauty with a reflector can give you stunning results. Reflectors are invaluable lighting tools as they can modify the light in a wide variety of ways. Reflectors can be used along with clamp lights to get the most lighting options possible. If you are working outside and do not have access to electricity for your clamp lights, reflectors will be your primary tool. If you know that you will have help during the shoot then an assistant can hold the reflector for you. You can also prop the reflector up on objects in the scene but holding it in place on windy days is a bit of challenge. Duct tape would come in handy for holding the reflector in place but be sure not to damage the reflector with the tape. You might even try bringing your light stands and attaching your reflector to the stand. Once you see how wonderful this simple piece of equipment is, you will never shoot without it again.

BACKDROPS If you have room to bring backdrops and a backdrop holder, bring them. By setting up a backdrop in the scene, you can hide unwanted information and add a professional quality to your images. Backdrops are to use both indoors and out. Setting up a backdrop outdoors will allow you to capture the beauty of natural light with the background of your choice. If you carry a variety of backdrops with you then you will have more options for selecting a backdrop that works best in the scene.

It is amazing what a simple reflector can do to the quality of light in your images. By bouncing light into shadow areas, reflectors will give your images a professional, sophisticated look.

TIP: Sometimes the best way to modify outdoor light is to filter the light that hits your subject. Cut out an opening in the largest piece of foam core board that you can find. Purchase material that is semi-transparent and stretch it over your foam core frame. Then place the filter between the light source and your subject. You will see an immediate change in the quality of light.

Skill builder

To understand just how amazing a simple reflector can be outdoors, take the reflector that you made and go outside with it. Find an object to photograph such as a chair, a planter or a still life of fruit that you have arranged on a table. If an individual is willing to sit for you, that would be even better. Experiment with the reflector to see how you can bounce the natural light from your reflector to your subject. Create a series of images that shows all of the different ways that the reflector can be used to modify the light that illuminates your subject.

Expert Advice: Capturing Personality & Getting Good Expressions

Sandy Puc, Owner, Expressions Photography

THE ULTIMATE GOAL: CAPTURING PERSONALITY

The most important factor in creating a great portrait is capturing expressions that display the personality of your subject. To capture great expressions, the environment where you take photographs should be relaxing and stress-free. The lighting, body language and pose of your subjects should look natural instead of forced. If the lighting is harsh or the pose looks uncomfortable it will disrupt the viewer's experience of the photograph.

GETTING GOOD EXPRESSIONS

My trick to getting good expressions is being playful with my subject. You must allow yourself to play games and be genuinely silly. Another trick is to use whimsical words and phrases that will evoke laughter. Give yourself permission to have fun without being self-conscious!

BUILD A RELATIONSHIP WITH THE SUBJECT

It is also important to try to establish a pleasant relationship with your subject. When photographing children be patient, prepare to bribe and pace your bribery. Don't promise the unseen. Have a gift purchased and wrapped before you begin to shoot. As you are photographing let the child examine the wrapped gift. Shoot some more and then let the child inspect it again. At the end of the shoot let them open the gift. A wrapped gift or a grab bag full of surprises that they can discover throughout the shoot will spark their attention and hold their concentration during the shoot.

I make adults and teens feel comfortable and at ease in front of the camera by talking with them and creating a comfortable relationship. Try to find common interests to discuss and most of all, be real. It sometimes helps to ask your subject to say things that you know will get them to laugh or let them take down their guard. I often ask my subjects to say "I am so good looking," it always makes them laugh.

PRACTICE MAKES PERFECT

To become a better portrait photographer you must practice, practice, practice and then make some mistakes; I've basically made every mistake in the book, in rapid succession. But each lesson translated into major improvements in my craft. It's ok to make mistakes, just learn from them and don't repeat them.

SANDY PUC has become an industry leader in children's photography, with recognition in multiple publications nationwide. Expressions Photography started in 1991 in a single room in Sandy's home and has since evolved to the present 5,000-square-foot building with eight different studio bays. Sandy has earned accolades in the portrait industry for creative marketing skills, business acumen and storybook artistry.

Every Picture Tells a Story

Great stories fill our minds with wonder, our hearts with emotion and our eyes with vivid images. To tell a vivid story, the storyteller has to recognize the significance of a moment in time, capture a telling mood, describe rich detail and see the extraordinary beauty within the experiences that make us human.

Photographers are visual storytellers, and every single photograph made tells a story about the moment captured and the photographer that captured it. By honing your visual storytelling skills you will be able to make photographs that tell a lifetime of stories.

So get your camera gear together and get out there; the world is full of stories just waiting to be told. Every photograph that you make has the potential to become a beautiful visual story that captures the poetry of living.

Hawaiian

Honeymoon by the sea

Life is not measured in the number of **breaths**......but in the moments that take *our breath away*

We spent two glorious weeks on the Big Island of Hawaii among the most amazing flora and fauna and deserted black- sand-beaches. A trip highlight was our 20 minute hikes down into the *Waipi'o Valley*, which connects three valleys, has no inroads to it and is heralded as the cradle of Hawaiian Civilization. Being there was akin to experiencing the Dawn of Time;

Moments That Tell It All

Every time that you take a photograph, you are making choices about what to photograph, when to photograph, how to photograph and where to photograph. Even before you raise the camera to your eye you have already made a complex series of decisions that will determine exactly how the photograph will look. Most of us make these split-second decisions without ever realizing that we have actually made them. But the moment you start recognizing the questions and making deliberate choices, your photographs will change. To capture moments that tell it all, you need to be a great observer, to identify the significance of the events unfolding in front of you, to visualize how you want the photographs to look, to get your equipment ready and to take the shot at just the right moment.

BE AN OBSERVER Before you begin shooting, take some time to observe all that is happening in the scene. Watch how people interact and behave. Consider which individuals might be more willing to be photographed. Look at the space and note areas that have interesting visual elements. Notice the light. Is it harsh or soft, warm or cool, fluorescent or tungsten? Is there a place within the space where the light is just perfect for making photographs? If there is an event going on, find out exactly what it is and why it is happening. Are there objects in the scene that are visually interesting and significant to the events taking place? If there are interesting objects, could they be used as props in a photograph? Walk around the site and take everything in; when you see something that catches your eye, go have a closer look.

IDENTIFY AND DESCRIBE THE EVENT'S CHARACTERISTICS

After you have done some detective work, begin to identify the significant and unique aspects of the events occurring. What you are looking for are images that depict the character of the place, the passion of the individuals in the scene and the energy of the moment. Make a mental list of some key words to describe the scene. Recently I photographed a family reunion. My list of key words included sumptuous food, running children, long conversations around the table, gifts, joy, young and old, laughter, a walk to the beach, admiration, exhausted children at the end of the day and tearful goodbyes. The words you use to identify and describe the event are a smart starting point for images that will reveal the significance of the moment.

I spent the afternoon watching the boys collecting shells and catching small fish. As the day went on, the evening light began to transform the scene into wonderful colors and I started photographing. I wanted to capture that great light and the boys "in the moment." I did not interrupt them as they played and kept my distance to avoid distracting them.

VISUALIZE KEY SHOTS With your list of key words start imagining images that you could make to illuminate those words. Food was the central element of this family reunion. An uncle, known for his cooking, had the outdoor grill full of meat and vegetables that he carefully tended. How about a close-up photograph of his hands flipping food on the smoking grill? A family friend brought a case of plums with green leaves still attached that were picked fresh from the backyard. How about a photograph of the friend walking in the door with the case of plums in her hands? The dinner table was three plastic tables placed together and a makeshift canopy of sheets was draped in the trees to cool the hot sun. Before everyone sits at the table to eat, could you photograph the tables in their makeshift environment with food ready to be eaten? Children sneaked small pieces of bread off the table and ate it as they ran around playing tag. How about taking one basket of bread, setting it on the table and asking the children to reach in to the basket as you photograph from above? There was a constant stream of plates heaped with food getting passed around the table. This photograph could be made from your seat with a slow shutter speed. As the bowl of salad comes your way, reach out and grab it as you take the photograph. With a slow shutter speed you could capture a blur. Every one of these descriptions could become a storytelling photograph; let your imagination and instincts run wild when considering ways to photograph them.

GETTING READY TO CAPTURE
THE TELLING MOMENTS Now that you have identified the event, the significance of the event and images that would describe the uniqueness of the event—get ready to shoot. Load your camera with film, select the lenses that you would like to use and check to see that your batteries are fully charged. Take some light-meter readings to get a sense of what the light is like and what your exposures need to be. Identify where the light is and anticipate where it will be as the day progresses. Look around the space and note terrific backdrops, colors, light and atmosphere.

A sweet and quiet captured moment was possible because the photographer was prepared, ready to shoot and sensitive to the significance of the moment. Photo: Tara Pakosta, Libertyville, Illinois

GO AND BE A PHOTOGRAPHER With camera in
hand, go explore the scene. Look through your camera and explore various camera angles. Take the photographs that you visualized making and be sure to capture others that pop up along the way. Because you have thoughtfully considered the event and image possibilities before you began to photograph, you will be better prepared to respond intuitively to changing situations while maintaining visual cohesiveness. Capture moments that unfold in front of the camera. Then make constructed images to tell the story by asking your subjects to pose for you or by making arrangements for the camera. Take shots that show the entire scene and then get as close as you can. Change lenses on occasion to see things from a new perspective. Pay attention to the photographs that excite you and respond by making a number of different versions of that subject. Remember to work with the depth of field and shutter speed to vary the visual dynamics in the images.

There are some situations, like a day at the pool, that give photographers more than one opportunity to capture a particular moment. Noah must have jumped off the diving board over 30 times. The repetition of this action gave me time to consider the best location to photograph from, the right lens to use, the optimal shutter speed to photograph with and the most interesting point of view. With all those issues worked out, capturing the moment was simply a matter of waiting for a memorable expression.

Mood Tells a Story

Photographs that are described as powerful often have one thing in common: a distinct and decisive mood. As human beings we are keenly aware of how images make us feel. Often our response is a "gut" reaction that identifies the mood precisely without us ever realizing exactly what in the photograph makes us feel this way. Skilled photographers who create images with distinct moods know exactly how to put images together to achieve an emotive response from the viewer. They use light, weather, visual dynamics and expressions like instruments in a symphony and combine them together to create music that moves us. It is such a pleasure to make photographs that establish a mood in such a way that inspires "ohs" and "aahs" from the viewer. Getting good at it is simply a matter of paying attention to how you feel, recognizing the elements of the scene that can be used to evoke a mood and putting it all together in the most evocative way.

Skilled and observant photographers use many different strategies for creating mood in photographs. The blue fog rolling across the surface of a lake echoes the somber feeling created by the composition and lone individual at the end of the dock. The sliver of brilliant light at the edge of a turbulent storm creates both tension and hope.

HOW LIGHT CREATES MOOD The quality of light in every photograph establishes a mood. Light streaming through a canopy of trees is ethereal. The setting sun that paints the sky in dramatic golds, reds and blues is magic. The edge of darkness that surrounds a street lamp illuminated at night is foreboding. The sizzling hot sun of midday is harsh, stark and intense. Pay attention to the emotional quality of light and make deliberate choices for what time of day to photograph and in what lighting conditions to photograph. Light is the most powerful visual mood creator. Use it thoughtfully and the emotional qualities that you seek will surface in the photographs you make.

HOW WEATHER CREATES MOOD The weather affects how we feel and is a terrific visual element that can add a distinctive mood to your photographs. Rain will change the color of everything to muted gray tones, softening contrast and color and evoking a somber mood. Falling snow can be graceful and peaceful or slicing and blue or dark gray. When the sun is out, snow can be intensely contrasty and too bright to look at without squinting. Snow in a photograph can make us feel cold, depressed or filled with joy. Stormy skies speak for themselves. With dramatic shafts of light and deep blue, gray and black clouds that loom and rumble in the distance, stormy skies can make us feel unsettled and anxious. Mist creates wonderful atmospheric qualities that inspire emotions. Mist is poetic, mysterious, obscuring, gentle and thick. It covers everything in a veil of silver lace and makes it shimmer.

Skill builder

Hone your ability to detect mood by spending some time looking through images made by photographic artists. As you see images that grab your attention, stop and look further. Scan your feelings and identify what thoughts filled your initial reaction. Find a number of words that describe the mood of the image and write them down. Then write down the categories of light, weather, visual dynamics and expression explored in these two pages. Look carefully at the image and list under these categories the exact details of the image that fit. In this exercise you are deconstructing the image and identifying the specific elements in the image that are creating the mood of the image. By practicing this exercise you will be teaching yourself to identify exactly how an image feels and the elements that the artist has used to make it feel a particular way. As you learn to see and understand how powerful images evoke a mood, you will be building the skills you need to capture mood in your own photographs.

TIP: When photographing in weather conditions that have any moisture at all, you must protect your camera from getting wet. I find it difficult to shoot with my camera covered in plastic and a hole cut out for the lens so I always look for cover. Shoot from a doorway, a window or inside a car. Find cover under a porch or an awning. And remember that where there is thunder there is lightning. No photograph is worth getting electrocuted.

THE VISUAL DYNAMICS OF MOOD

The way a photograph is put together can be used to evoke a mood in the image. Deliberate choices made in the composition, color and texture, point of view, framing strategies and scale can underscore any emotive quality that you are trying to capture. To create a sense of serenity, choose an uncluttered and central composition with a shallow depth of field to obscure the background. Find a point of view that feels natural to what the human eye sees and does not distort the image. Look for blues, greens and browns with uncomplicated textures. Look for monochromatic scenes that have a dominant color. To create a feeling of chaos, shoot from above to distort the sense of scale and confuse the viewer. Look for sharp angles and dramatic curves to fill the frame. Create a composition with the frame tilted and off center. Look for hot and vibrant colors that compete with each other in the scene. Paying attention to how the visual dynamics in your photographs can be manipulated to achieve a particular mood will help you to establish your own personal visual style.

HOW EXPRESSIONS DEPICT MOOD

When a photograph has individuals in it, the most significant aspect of the image that determines the mood is the look on their faces. Viewers will always have a direct and immediate response to the facial expressions that are captured. If someone is laughing, we will laugh too. If someone is crying, we feel sad too. If someone looks serious, we have concern for what might have happened. The expression of the individual photographed tells it all. Be sensitive to the mood of those individuals that you are working with. Rather than asking them to smile, as we so often do, capture the mood that they are in. Let their feelings show in the image and your photographs will have more emotional complexity.

Engaging expressions can get lost in an image when the photographer is simply not standing close enough to the subject. Get close and down low enough to become eye level with your subject. Then when great expressions happen you will be right there to capture them.

Skill builder

Practice and expand your ability to create expressive and distinctive moods in your photographs. Give yourself the assignment of shooting a series of images or an entire roll of film that captures one mood in a variety of ways. Practice capturing that mood by photographing specific qualities of light, composition and expression that reinforce those feelings.

Details Inform the Story

Important elements in any great visual story are the details. Details provide specific information that can inform our understanding of the way things seem. Details also serve to transform our understanding of the way things are by showing us images we have never seen before. When we create photographs of very small things and make them larger than life we have the unique opportunity to observe and scrutinize objects in ways that the human eye is simply not able to do. Capturing the details photographically allows the viewer time to contemplate objects in new ways. In photographic storytelling details offer a welcome emotional and visual shift in the rhythm of more predictable and traditional kinds of images. Every photographic story should include details that give the viewer a better sense of the subject and provide the photographer with opportunities to stretch his or her creativity into seeing the world in new ways.

Photographic details are like spices in cooking that add depth and interest to a wonderful meal. Detail images are often created to support a larger grouping of images. But great detail images can stand alone on their own merit. The striped shells that my son collected on a hike matched the stripes in his shirt creating visual harmony in the image. This detail also shows my son's curiosity with nature. Details do not always have to be small things. This field of red poppies in Italy makes a terrific stand-alone image.

Skill builder

For every event or place that you photograph, create two or three detail photographs. Look for images that capture elements of the event or place that define the uniqueness or significance of the story.

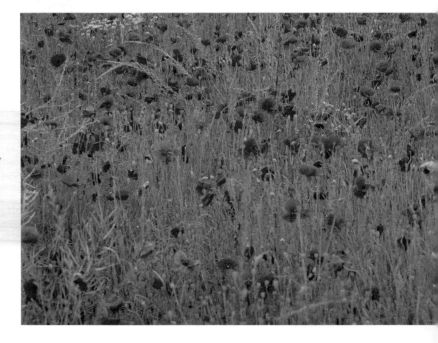

EQUIPMENT FOR CAPTURING DETAIL

Every lens has a minimum focusing distance that can capture sharp detail. Standard lenses for 35mm cameras are not capable of photographing any closer than 2 to 4 feet from the subject. With standard lenses photographers can certainly make detail shots but they will be limited to how close they can get. Most standard lenses will work just fine to photograph a platter of roasted turkey and apple-sausage stuffing placed in the center of the Thanksgiving table. But to photograph the red skin of an apple, speckled with tiny white marks that transform into a galaxy of stars, will require a specially designed lens. Macro lenses are the easiest lenses to use for getting really close to objects. They can be purchased as fixed-length lenses like 55mm or specialty zoom lenses. Sometimes it is necessary to use a tripod and a cable release when you are working on close-up images to keep the camera steady as images are captured.

CLOSE-UP TECHNIQUES FOR CAPTURING DETAIL

The most important consideration in capturing detail is depth of field. The closer you get to the subject, the narrower your depth of field will be. Because of this it is important to focus your images carefully. If you want to get the most depth of field possible, you need to adjust your aperture setting to f/16 or f/22 and place your camera on a tripod to photograph if the shutter speed is going to be slower than 1/60th of a second. Small objects are easily moved by wind, so pay attention to blurring that can be caused by even the slightest gust. With small objects movement is magnified; be sure to stabilize your camera on the tripod and use a cable release so the action of releasing the shutter will not cause camera shake.

TIP: Use a reflector to help you light those all-important detail shots. While it is easy enough to make your own reflector out of foam core, a professional, store-bought reflector has many advantages. Professional reflectors can fold up to be quite compact and often have both a white and a silver side for increased light-bouncing capabilities. If your reflector is very portable and easy to use, you will be more likely to carry it with you all the time. A professional reflector is worth every penny that you might spend on it because the results of using one are outstanding.

Photographing details offers the photographer an opportunity to be inventive about his or her images. Fountains are typically photographed from a distance that locates the fountain in a particular space. So break the rules and get really close; the details are just fascinating. Getting close to unusual and even ordinary things can create surprising results. The arrangement of fruit in this fruit tart was a work of art in itself but the tart was located in a glass case at a storefront window. To make this photograph I asked for permission and held my camera right on the case to reduce glare and to fill the entire frame.

Playtime: The Story of Childhood

Watching children play is one of the greatest joys of being a parent. When children play they become the characters that they invent. They take on the character's voice, gestures and language. They rummage through dressers and closets to find clothing and accessories that transform them from little boys and girls to superheroes, dinosaurs, kittens, moms and dads. They construct elaborate setups to play house in, to rocket to the moon and to rescue cats from trees or people out of dangerous situations. When children play, time stands still as they are transported to new places and experience wild adventures. Every parent with a camera has photographed his or her child at play hoping to capture the wonderful and precious moments that playtime truly is. Turn your hopes of capturing these moments into confidence that you will create photographs that reveal the essence of childhood.

GETTING WHAT YOU WANT WITHOUT GETTING IN THE WAY

It is useful to consider two different approaches to photographing a child fully engaged in hosting a formal dinner party at Barbie's house. The first approach is to photograph from the outside looking in. Do not disturb the child and photograph quietly and unobtrusively from the sidelines. Use of a variety of lenses will allow you to keep some distance while photographing. A wide-angle lens will help you capture the entire scene. Switching to a zoom or telephoto lens will allow you to stay right where you are as you make detail or close-up shots. The less you walk around the room, the more unobtrusive you will be.

After you have taken a variety of shots from the sidelines, consider getting into the game. Go put on a fancy necklace and a scarf then knock on Barbie's door and let her know that you have arrived to photograph the party. Be sure to thank her for inviting a photographer. Now you are a player in the game and will be able to photograph from an insider's point of view. As you sit on the floor playing with your child, take a moment every now and then to photograph. On the floor you will be able to photograph playtime from a different point of view and to create more close-up shots that describe detail, facial expressions and constructions that your child has created. As the photographer at the dinner party, you might want to ask the hostess to pose for a few photographs. Don't forget that photographers also photograph rescues, time travel, veterinarians and paleontologists.

TIP: Get kids involved in creating photographs of playtime. Tell them that you want to photograph them playing, then ask them to create constructions or entire scenes that you can photograph together. My lads love to create dioramas of dinosaurs or backyard forts to be photographed.

Photographing children at play offers fantastic opportunities to capture wonderful moments of expressive gestures, dynamite facial expressions, contagious laughter and the creativity of childhood constructions. To photograph playtime, photographers need to strike a delicate balance between getting into the middle of things to capture the moment and staying just far enough away so that the moment is not disturbed. It requires patience, timing and an ability to work quickly. But most of all, photographing children at play requires you to have fun too.

The amazing thing about young children is their sense of wonder in the smallest of things. Seeing the world from the point of view of your child can help to capture terrific moments and splendid visual arrangements. To make this photograph I was lying flat on my stomach in the sand and had to jump up more than once to keep him from putting handfuls of sand in his mouth.

TIMING IS EVERYTHING With a child at play, timing can make or break a great photograph. An element of timing applies to both the subject of the child playing and the photographer's decision of when to take the photograph. A child at play may be engaged in the activity for three minutes or an hour. You simply never know. It is a good idea to always have your camera gear ready to go at all times so you won't miss the most exciting three minutes of playtime that your child has ever had. Knowing the games that your child loves to play will help you to anticipate how long the playtime will be. Longer playtimes will afford you more opportunities to photograph.

COMPENSATING FOR CHILDRENS' UNPREDICTABILITY Children are unpredictable, and getting a few great shots sometimes requires shooting an entire roll of film. To increase the percentage of successful photographs, pre-focusing will allow you to quickly respond to any opportunity. To pre-focus simply look through the camera and focus in the area that you think the next shot will be. You can save time by observing the activity through your viewfinder so that when you see something that you want to photograph, the camera is already at your eye. Look for defining moments that capture the significance of the activity. Look for moments where the child's facial expression, gestures and surroundings come together in the most exciting way.

CAPTURING THE PLAYTIME MAGIC Children have incredibly creative spirits that can transform a wooden kitchen spoon into a knight's shield, a magic wand or a fishing pole. Their imaginations are limitless and their ability to step into fascinating worlds with body and soul is inspiring. As children grow older they become interested in other kinds of play and the magic of complete transformation is gone.

Beyond photographing children while they are playing, take some time to photograph the objects that they create—sand castles, forts made of boxes, a crumpled skirt made of foil tied around a teddy bear and building-block airplanes that transform into spaceships and submarines. These wonderful creations symbolize childhood and can reveal the unique personality of your child.

Travel Photography: Lasting Stories of Adventure

Who doesn't take a camera with them when they travel? To photograph a trip is to save some of the most thrilling moments that we might experience in a lifetime. Most people who photograph when they travel instinctively use their cameras to capture all the things that are different than what we see at home. Traveling gives us opportunities to see historical sites, experience new foods, shop for things we can't find at home, observe new fashions, interact with strangers, see new landscapes and admire stunning architecture. When we travel we open up our eyes and our minds in new ways. We become much better observers because our sense of sight, smell, sound and touch are piqued. Great travel photographs capture the essence of place and the wonder and excitement that we feel when we travel. Making photographs that get below the surface of your travel experience requires you to be well-prepared and thoughtful about the photographs you make.

> **TIP:** When you know where you are going to travel, take some time to hit the books. As with any subject in photography, the more you know about it, the better the photographs will be. Research the history of the place you are going to. Historical information will allow you to see the significance and symbolic potential of architecture, monuments and locations within the context of history. Research the culture to gain insight into the defining characteristics of the people, the politics, the customs, the artwork and the local cuisine.

The Grand Canal in Venice is the source of many famous paintings. Its charm and magic can be captured with inventive points of view and unusual light.

TRAVEL COMFORTABLY When traveling you will encounter a wide variety of unpredictable shooting situations. While you want to be prepared to photograph everything, you need to be realistic about what you can travel with comfortably. How much stuff you want to carry should be the starting point for packing your gear. Fill your camera bag with all the gear you want to travel with. Take a long walk around the neighborhood and see how it feels. If the bag is too heavy, carrying your camera gear around and taking photographs will be a chore. Make sure that you are comfortable with the weight of your bag. Being comfortable and mobile is much more important than carrying that extra 300mm lens. Make sure that you have a comfortable camera bag. I prefer to travel with a backpack-style camera bag. With a backpack I can have my hands free to shoot while the rest of my gear is on my back. A backpack also saves your body the aches and pains of carrying a heavy shoulder bag. The disadvantage of a backpack-style camera bag is that every time you need to change a roll of film or a lens, you have to take the bag off your back, get the things you need and then put it back—which can slow you down. A great advantage of a shoulder bag is the ease and speed of getting in and out of the bag; you simply shift the bag from the side to the front and everything you need is right there.

WHAT GEAR SHOULD YOU TAKE? I have always traveled with both my SLR and a point-and-shoot camera. With a point-and-shoot you can photograph quickly and capture fleeting moments. An SLR will allow you much greater visual control over your images. If you have an SLR and a point-and-shoot, I would recommend that you bring both. If you have only one camera, the choice of what to bring is easy. If you have interchangeable lenses, I would consider bringing a normal, a wide-angle and a telephoto lens. If you don't want to carry that many pieces of equipment or that much weight, one zoom lens that can go from wide to normal to telephoto will give you everything that you need. Putting filters on your camera lenses is a good way to protect your lenses from damage. You should purchase a skylight filter for every lens you have. If you have a polarizing filter, bring it along; it could come in handy when photographing through windows when glare is bouncing around in the scene. Consider bringing a tripod and a cable release. I carry a mini-tripod that I can set up on a tabletop or other surface; it's lightweight, easy to use and compact for travel. Lens-cleaning tissue will come in handy to keep your lens clean. Bring a flash if you have one. Extra camera and flash batteries are a must. Make sure you carry three sets of each. Purchase all the film that you plan on shooting before you leave. Buying film in other countries or from souvenir shops is much more expensive and choices are always limited. For those of you shooting with digital cameras, be sure to bring additional memory and batteries.

KEEPING YOUR CAMERA SAFE

Having your camera stolen is the last thing that you want to have happen while you are traveling. If you have a habit of setting your camera bag down while you shoot it is time to make a change. You should keep your camera bag on you at all times. To protect your camera from the bumps and bangs that are part of the travel experience, be sure that your camera bag is well-padded. If you are the type that has turned one of your own bags into a camera bag, then I highly suggest that you leave it at home. Camera bags are specifically designed to provide the kind of padding that your camera needs to stay safe.

PASSING SECURITY CHECKPOINTS

Traveling by plane requires you to send all of your equipment through X-ray machines. Most X-ray machines do not affect normal-speed films. Very high-speed film, like ASA3200, can become fogged with too many passes through X-ray scanners. There was a time when you could put your film in a lead bag and send it through X-ray or have your film hand-inspected, but those days are over. You will be asked to put your film and everything else you have through the machine. You might even be asked to take your camera out and show that it is working and has not been modified. A security official may even look through all your lenses. So go with the flow; you have no choice.

Looking back at this Italian village from a pier captures the beauty of this tiny seaport town.

GIVE YOURSELF MINI ASSIGNMENTS

A productive way to photograph your travels is to give yourself miniature assignments to shoot along the way. Giving yourself mini assignments will add cohesiveness and structure to your images. It also provides a way of sifting through all the visual imagery that bombards the travel experience. As you are doing your cultural and historical research, pay attention to the images that you see. Having an understanding of what things will look like when you get there will give you a chance to brainstorm some mini assignments before you go. Make a list of these assignments and write down some of the images that you can envision taking. Here are some assignment ideas to get you started: food, fashion, tourists, transportation, storefronts, monuments, architecture, light, texture, color, churches, people, parks, local crafts and artisans, markets, door knockers, windows, festivals, shadows, gardens and ruins. Choose assignments that will help you to uncover the distinct qualities of the people and the places you travel to.

Rather than photograph the entire building, I focused instead on the dome and these sculptures. Capturing an interesting and visually dynamic piece of the whole can create an image that actually says more rather than less.

The Photo Essay

Photo essays are the ultimate form of storytelling in photography. They are carefully conceived and created with the goal of telling visual stories that enlighten, inform and move the viewer. As a scrapbooker, you may be somewhat familiar with the concept of photo essays through the series of photographs you take to document specific events. A deeper look into the art form will bring more thorough photographic stories into your scrapbooks. Shooting for a photo essay requires the photographer to wear many hats at once as he or she goes from shooting portraits and close-ups to environmental shots and significant moments. Everything that you have learned in this book has given you the skills you need to create technically solid and visually dynamic photo essays. All you need now is a better understanding of what makes a great photo essay and practical advice on how to put one together.

THE INGREDIENTS OF A
GREAT PHOTO ESSAY

Great photo essays are like great novels. There is a theme, characters and an element of time. There is a beginning, middle and an ending. There is a point of view, descriptive details, distinctive moods and defining moments. There is a sense of the environment and a sequence of events. Every great photo essay pulls all of these key elements together in a specific visual order designed to tell exciting and interesting stories.

PHOTO ESSAY THEMES

What separates a photo essay from a group of photographs is a theme or an idea that you set out to explore. Many people have created photo essays based on the popular theme of "A Day in the Life." This idea has been used to photograph everything from a day in the life of a child to a day in the life of America. Any event or activity has the potential to become an exciting photo essay. Here is a list of photo essay themes to get you started: holidays, family reunions,

football games, weddings, pregnancy, the first day of school, a birthday party, graduation, a trip to the zoo, a vacation, first haircut, a hike in the mountains, spring, Grandma's cooking, house projects and prom night, just to name a few.

DEPICTING THE PASSAGE OF TIME

Photo essays have elements of time that determine when the shooting begins and ends. Oftentimes the theme itself sets the time frame. "A Day in the Life" creates a structure for shooting any living subject throughout a single day. Photo essays can show events that last a couple of hours—like football games, family reunions and a Thanksgiving meal. Other essay themes like weddings, holidays and vacations can occur over days. Some photographers have taken on themes that need to be shot over the course of many years like a changing neighborhood or couples growing old together. Creating a photo essay requires a commitment of time.

PORTRAYING THE STORY'S CHARACTERS

Shooting for a photo essay often requires making casual and formal portraits of main characters. When you see an opportunity to photograph the main characters, begin photographing without interrupting them so that you can capture natural moments. Then ask the subjects if they would be willing to pose for you and subtly direct the images so that you can capture that natural moment and have more control over how the image looks.

The three images on this page focus on the two main characters of the photo essay and are the beginning of the photo essay. Together these three images have a similar composition that underscores the passing of time and gives the viewer a chance to get to know the main characters of the photo essay.

DETERMINE A POINT OF VIEW

Novelists create stories that are told from a specific point of view. Stories are told through the eyes of the writer, a main character, an outside observer or even the family dog. Consider the point of view in your photo essay. As the photographer, you are a "fly on the wall" observing and recording what you see. A clever way to make unusual photographs within your story is to shift the point of view from yourself to another character in the story you are photographing. Imagine what the events might look like from the point of view of a child or the bride-to-be. From a child's point of view you would shoot images from a low vantage point that is always looking up. From a bride's point of view, bridesmaids handing you your veil would surround you. Changing your point of view is a unique way to create inventive images for your story.

ADD INFORMATION WITH DEFINING DETAILS

Photographing details is another superb way to add information and creative possibilities to your essay. With every theme there are objects that are symbolic of the event. A close-up shot of a wedding band says "newlywed," a photograph of a mud-covered jersey number says "athlete" while a pumpkin pie says "Thanksgiving." These seemingly simple images have terrific graphic qualities that add to the visual diversity of the final grouping of images.

ENERGIZE THE ESSAY BY CAPTURING MOOD

Every theme has a distinctive mood that should be captured in your photo essay. Creating images that establish the mood of an activity or event gets to the heart of the matter and energizes the essay with emotion. Look for expressions, gestures, body language and significant moments between individuals. Consider the mood established by the quality of light or atmospheric conditions.

SHOW THE DEFINING MOMENTS

Photo essays rely upon images that define the significance of the event. These images are essential because they serve to tell the viewer exactly what the purpose of the gathering is. For a wedding, a defining moment would be the kiss at the altar or the cutting of the cake. Blowing out the candles on a birthday cake defines a moment. Mortarboards soaring through the air define a graduation. You will find that as soon as you begin thinking about defining moments for the event you are photographing, many images will come to mind. When you anticipate what those shots will be, you can plan out the equipment that you will need to make the shot, the place that you will need to be when the moment occurs and you will have a good idea of when to expect it. Being prepared for these shots will help you make fantastic defining moments.

FIND THE BEGINNING, MIDDLE AND END

Almost every single event has a beginning, middle and an end. Paying close attention to these aspects of your theme will give your photo essay clear starting and ending points. Most people think of the starting whistle as the beginning of the football game. But the game begins the moment your football player gets out of bed. Perhaps he eats a protein- and carbohydrate-packed breakfast of eggs, bacon and pancakes on game day. Then he gets dressed into his sweats and takes a walk around the block to clear his head. He goes to the field and meets his teammates in the locker room and changes for the game. After warm-ups and introductions, the game begins. All of the preparations that led up to the event offer great opportunities for creating unique images. And when the referee blows the whistle at the end of the game, the event is not yet over. Sometimes the most interesting images made in a photo essay are the activities and preparations that occur before and after the event.

As the tension of delivery builds, these three images capture the mood of individuals in the room and the defining moments of exerted energy and the baby's arrival. These images represent the middle of the photo essay.

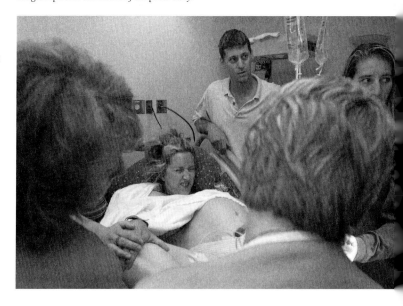

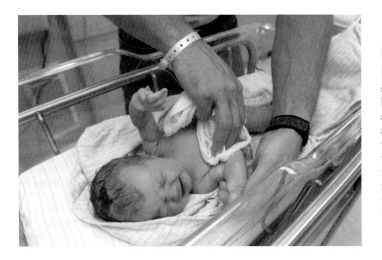

PHOTOGRAPH THE DEFINING ENVIRONMENT Environmental photographs capture a sense of place and add depth to the story. Environments are significant because they influence the quality of light, create a formal or casual atmosphere and provide opportunities for interesting backdrops and visual elements that can be incorporated into compositions. A wedding party at a country club looks and feels very different from a wedding party at a nature center. In this case the choice of environment tells us quite a lot about the personalities and interests of the newlyweds. With all photo essay themes it is important to describe the setting with environmental shots because the setting influences the tone of the event itself.

EDITING YOUR PHOTO ESSAY Editing is one of the most important aspects of putting together a successful photo essay. The first and easiest step is to get rid of all the images that are not technically strong. Even if you love the image but the photograph is underexposed, it has to go. Images that have technical problems detract attention from the superior photographs. Lay all the images out on a table and begin grouping them into the following categories: characters; descriptive details; captured mood; defining moments, time and environment. If you have other categories of images that you shot, create a grouping of those as well. Within each category look for the two or three most visually dynamic and effective images and place those at the top of the group. Now collect those visually dynamic "best of category images" and set them aside. Take all the other images from your shooting and put them away. You now have a final edit.

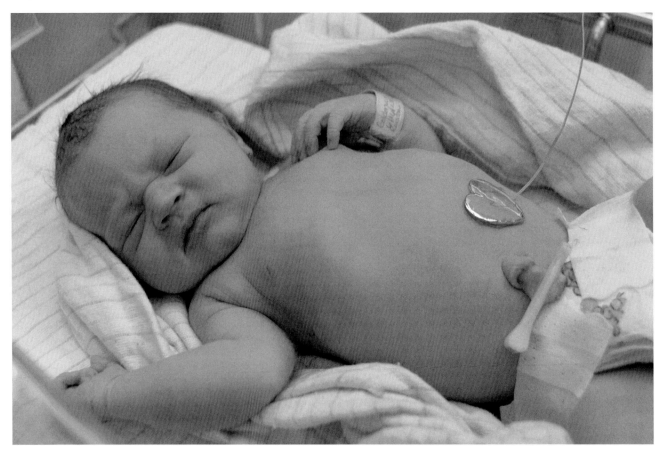

These images of the newborn baby were edited from over 20 images that showed close-ups of the baby and the baby being cleaned, measured and weighed. This edit of two images captures the essence of the image series by showing the father gently cleaning the baby and a close-up of the beautiful newborn resting peacefully.

SEQUENCING YOUR ESSAY'S IMAGES

There are many ways to sequence images in a photo essay. Sequences can be based upon a chronology of events. They can be sequenced based on visual dynamics like color, scale and composition. They can be sequenced by point of view or in categories like details, environment and characters. Think of the final grouping of images as one composition that needs to have strong visual dynamics. Consider the sequence's rhythm. It is not uncommon to make a pattern of arrangements such as vertical-vertical-vertical-horizontal-vertical-vertical-vertical-horizontal or detail-detail-mo-ment-detail-detail-moment. To create awesome sequences, spend time arranging and rearranging your edited group of images together. After you have experimented with the sequence, choose two or three that you like the most. Then take one of those three and arrange it in a safe place that you have to walk by often. Live with it for a day and see if the sequence still holds up over time. After you have given all three a test of time, one will surely stand out over the others. Sequencing is one of the most exciting aspects of putting a photo essay together because you finally get to see how the story turns out.

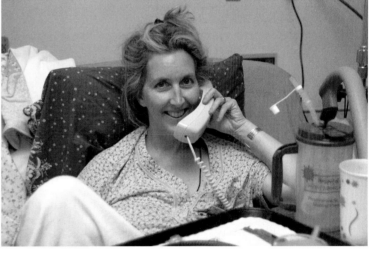

This group of images represents the end of the photo essay. With phone calls, photographs and sheer joy, the subjects reveal the excitement of the arrival of this new baby through the expressions and actions of family members. The final image of the tiny baby's hand in her father's hands helps to end the photo essay in such a way that reveals a sense of the preciousness of this new gift and the family that will cherish the new arrival.

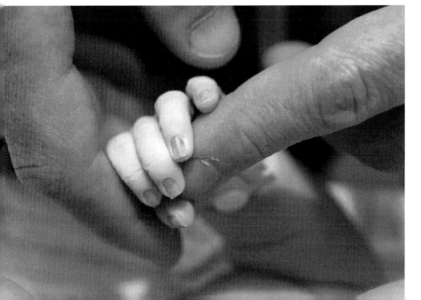

Making Your Photographs Even Better

I commend you for reading this book. You are clearly committed to making stunning photographs, and I have no doubt that you will. Reading books, practicing your skills and paying close attention to how you photograph will go a long way toward helping you to become a better photographer. If you want to take your technical and creative skills even further, here are some helpful ways to continue improving your work.

EVALUATE YOURSELF AND YOUR IMAGES

Every time you photograph is a learning opportunity, so take some time to evaluate the accomplishments and problems in your work. After every shoot, take a careful look at the images you made. Start with images that have technical problems and identify what went wrong. It is absolutely true that we learn the most from our mistakes. Then identify the successful photographs in the group. Excellent photographs work on many levels at once. They are perfectly exposed, have exciting visual dynamics, there are clear points to the images, they have a distinct emotional quality and the subject matter is interesting. Select images from your shoot that have as many of these qualities as possible; this selection should be your most successful images. Now take some time to acknowledge why and how the images are successful. With every roll of film or digital memory card, you should give yourself the challenge of solving a problem that you encountered. To improve your technique, choose one image from the roll that has technical difficulty and identify what you should have done to make it perfect. Then choose an image that was not successful for reasons other than technique and identify what you could have done to make it better. If you do this with every roll of film you shoot, in no time you will be solving problems as they arise in front of the camera rather than after the images are shot.

Taking time to evaluate the success and problems in the photographs you make will help you to become a better photographer.

GET FEEDBACK FROM FAMILY AND FRIENDS

Getting feedback can dramatically improve your photographic work. Ask someone you know and respect to take a look at some of your photographs. Take a small grouping of your best ones and lay them out for your friend to see. Do not say anything about the photographs: no comments about whom the individuals are, where they were taken or for what reason. You don't want to influence the comments that your friend is going to make. Ask your friend to answer the following questions for each photograph and listen very carefully to the answers: What is the photograph about? What is the point of the photograph? Does it make you feel anything? Is the subject matter interesting? What is not working about the photograph? Be sure that you don't interrupt or explain a thing, or answer questions that your friend asks; just let him or her talk while you listen. You can learn a great deal from how people respond to these questions. By comparing what you think your images are all about to what others see them as, you will know if your intentions were communicated. Knowing how to make photographs that communicate to the viewer exactly what you have in mind is the key to making power-ful photographs.

SEEK INSPIRATION FROM INSPIRING SOURCES

Books are a fantastic place to find inspiration. Every library has a section on photography, so take advantage of this resource to get your creative juices flowing. Look at everything—commercial photography, photojournalism and fine-art photography. Look at how photographers put images together, capture moments and create constructions for the camera. Look at the subject matter they choose to shoot. Look at the techniques they use and the style they develop in their work. There are also some wonderfully inspiring books out there that explore the lives and the passion of famous photographers such as Edward Weston, Diane Arbus and Ansel Adams. Looking at remarkable photographs and reading about photographers who centered their lives on making photographs will inspire your own images to be remarkable and your commitment to make powerful photographs even stronger.

Expert Advice: Honing Your Peripheral Vision
Tory Read, Documentary Photographer

HONE YOUR PERIPHERAL VISION

Many photographers fall into the trap of creating photographs of events and moments that are not surprising because they capture the scene in ways that we have all seen before. To get beyond cliché images, you need to ask yourself what is happening in the other room, away from the main action. While the anniversary party is in full swing, are the kids upstairs building some terrific construction? Is someone in the kitchen getting the cake ready? What is happening on the porch or in the back yard? As the photographer, you need to hone your peripheral vision and be aware of everything that is going on.

PREDICT WHERE THE ACTION WILL BE

Anticipating what is going to happen next is a big part of making great photographs. You have to be "in the moment" of the photograph you are making, but you also have to be thinking about what might happen in 10 seconds, 10 minutes or an hour. Consider ahead of time where you should be when certain things happen. Sometimes it is best to be right in the middle of things and sometimes it is best to be on the periphery. Be unobtrusive. If you are getting in the way too often, or if your flash is bothering everyone, you will have to make some changes. Keep in mind that even experts miss shots and significant moments; it is simply a part of the challenge of photographing.

BECOME AN EVENT PHOTOGRAPHER

A great way to build your skills is to start by photographing a child's party. Do not try to build your skills at a party for your own child. You will have too many responsibilities to tend to, and it will be difficult to concentrate on making photographs. Put yourself in a situation where there is a lot of activity and the people that you are photographing are more concerned with what they are doing rather than what you are doing. Imagine that you are shooting photographs for someone who was unable to attend the party. Your images should describe who, what, when, where, how and why of the event. When you are comfortable photographing an event centered around children, move on to photographing an event centered on adults.

TORY READ is a documentary photographer with a passion for telling intimate stories about people, places and cultures meeting the challenges of life in a world in rapid transition. Born and raised in New York, Tory has been a professional photographer and writer since she earned her M.A. in journalism at the University of Missouri School of Journalism in 1991. After graduate school, she started her career as a photojournalist for The Oakland Tribune and the Associated Press in San Francisco. Tory's commitment to photography and community has resulted in the development of community-based photography projects in urban and rural neighborhoods. Her photographic work with communities has attracted many sponsors, including the Colorado Council on the Arts, the National Endowment for the Arts, the United States Department of Justice and the Denver Foundation. See more of Tory's work on the Internet at www.toryread.com.

Sunday School; Uafato, Samoa. Archival Inkjet Print. 2004 © Tory Read. All rights reserved.

Glossary

Additive color mixing Red, green and blue light to create a full spectrum of color.

Aperture Located in the lens, the aperture is an adjustable opening or diaphragm that allows a measured amount of light into the camera.

Aperture-priority mode An operating mode that allows the photographer to select the aperture while the camera selects the shutter speed.

Auto focus A camera function that automatically selects and adjusts the focus for each image photographed.

Background The area of the scene that is located in the farthest part of the scene.

Backlighting Back lighting is light that comes from behind the subject causing an extreme lighting condition.

Backlighting compensation mode An operating mode on the camera that adjusts the light meter to produce a more accurate exposure in back-lit situations reducing the possibility for a silhouette image to occur.

Brightness How light or dark an image appears to be.

C-41 The chemical process used to develop color-negative film.

CD-R Recordable compact disc that can be recorded onto once. R stands for Read.

CD-RW Recordable compact disc that can be recorded onto many times. RW stands for Read-Write.

Cable release A cable that attaches to the shutter-release button on the camera that is designed to reduce camera shake caused by depressing the shutter-release button by hand.

Camera The camera is a device that captures light reflecting off of an object and records that light onto light-sensitive media.

Candid portrait A candid or casual portrait is a photograph of an individual that reveals a more natural pose, shows an individual engaged in an activity or captures an individual who is not making eye contact with the camera.

CMYK (Cyan, Magenta, Yellow and Black) Refers to the subtractive color theory and inks used in digital printing.

Color balance Refers to the relationship of colors in an image. Good color balance indicates that there is no apparent color bias or unusual colorcast in the image.

Color contrast Color contrast is created when complementary colors, colors that are opposite of each other on the color wheel, are combined together.

Color harmony Grouping of colors that create harmony. Harmonic colors are found next to each other on the color wheel.

Compact point-and-shoot Fully automatic camera that is easy to use, small, lightweight and portable.

Comparative scale The purposeful placement of one object next to another to establish a size comparison.

Composition The arrangement of objects in the frame.

Compression A digital process that reduces the size and quality of a digital image.

Contrast The difference between the dark areas and light areas in an image.

Daylight-balanced film Film designed to reproduce accurate color in daylight conditions.

Dedicated flash A flash unit that is usually made by the camera manufacturer and is designed to work in the hot shoe of your camera or with a special dedicated cable.

Depth of field The area of sharp focus in a photographic image.

Digital camera Cameras that use image-sensor chips to capture images in pixels and then store the images in memory.

Dominant color A scene or situation that has one primary color.

E-6 The chemical process used to develop color-slide film.

Exposure The range of detailed visual information captured on film or in pixels.

Exposures Indicates the number of frames or images that can be shot on one roll of film.

File size The amount of information contained in a digital image that indicates how large or small the image is and how much detail the image has.

Fill flash A technique of combining flash with ambient light to fill in the shadow areas of the subject.

Film Light-sensitive media that records the image created in the camera.

Film speed A numerical measurement that identifies how sensitive the film is to light.

Filters Specially designed optical accessories that screw directly onto the lens to modify and enhance the way images look.

Flash A built-in or attachable light source for your camera.

Foreground The area of the scene that is closest to the viewer.

Formal portrait A formal portrait is a photograph that is directed by the photographer to depict an individual that is looking into the camera and is positioned in a purposeful pose.

Frame-within-a-frame A compositional strategy that transforms objects and architectural elements into framing devices that surround the subject matter.

Front lighting Front lighting occurs when the direction of the light comes from behind the photographer and falls on the front of the subject.

F-stop A number that indicates the size of the aperture opening, such as f/2 or f/16.

Gray card An aid used to create a more accurate light-meter reading. The middle gray tone on the card represents an average tone between black and white and is the tone that the camera strives to reproduce in an exposure.

Hard drive The mechanism in the computer that stores data.

Hard light Light quality created when the light creates intense and contrasty bright and dark areas.

Horizon line The line created in the scene where the land and the sky meet.

Hot shoe The unit on your camera that is designed to couple with a flash unit.

Image formats Specific attributes assigned to a digital image that modifies the the image and allows the file to be used in a variety of digital applications.

Input Refers to getting images into the computer and devices designed to getting images into the computer such as scanners.

Interpolate A computer process that adds or deletes information in a digital image based on approximation.

ISO A numerical rating of the film's sensitivity to light.

K-14 The chemical process used to develop Kodachrome film.

Landscape mode An operating mode designed for photographing landscapes that reproduces images with a long depth of field.

Light meter The mechanism in the camera that measures the light in the scene and suggests an aperture opening and shutter-speed combination that will produce the best exposure.

Long exposure An exposure that requires the camera's shutter to remain open for an extended period of time. Most often used at night or in low-light situations.

Macro lens A macro lens is designed to photograph objects up close.

Manual/automatic flash unit A non-dedicated flash unit that connects to your camera via the hot shoe or with a synchronization cable.

Manual mode An operating mode that requires the photographer to adjust both the aperture and shutter speed to create a correct exposure.

MHz (megahertz) A measurement of the speed of the computer processor.

Middle ground The area of the scene that covers the middle of the image.

Monitor The screen of the computer.

Negative film Film that reproduces a negative or reversal of the original image.

Normal exposure Full range of detail in the highlights and shadow areas with a smooth transition of tones throughout the image.

Normal lens For 35mm cameras, a 50mm or 55mm lens that reproduces the scene without distortion.

Operating modes A variety of camera functions used to determine the exposure of the film given various shooting situations.

Operating system The software that makes the computer function.

Output Refers to devices designed to take images out of the computer such as a printer.

Overexposure An exposure that is caused by too much light reaching the film resulting in a very light image with little detail in the highlights.

Photo collage An image that is made up of a number of photographic images that have been physically cut and pasted together to create one image.

Photomontage A seamless arrangement or layering of many photographic images into one image.

Pixels Are the smallest bits of information contained in a digital image.

Point of view The location or position that the photographer chooses to make the photograph from.

Portrait mode An operating mode designed for photographing people that reproduces images with a shallow depth of field.

PPI (pixels per inch) The exact number of pixels in one inch of a digital image.

Print film Film that reproduces a negative image that is used for making prints.

Printer An output device designed to print digital information.

Program mode An operating mode indicated with a "P" for programmed exposure that automatically adjusts the camera to select both the correct shutter speed and aperture opening to achieve a correct exposure.

RAM (random access memory) The short-term memory that stores information about a digital file that is in use at the time.

Recycle time The amount of time that it takes energy to build back up in the flash after the flash has been fired.

Red eye The red color of in individual's eyes captured in a photographic image that is caused by the flash output bouncing off the retinal blood vessels in the back of the eye.

Remote control A transmitting and receiving unit built into some cameras that allows the photographer to remotely trigger the camera into taking a photograph.

Resolution Resolution refers to the amount of detail captured in a digital image.

RGB (Red, Green, Blue) Refers to additive color.

Rule of thirds A system for composing images that uses a grid of lines to section the image into nine equal rectangles and places the subject at any of the four intersecting lines of the grid.

Scale Scale is the size of objects in the scene that is informed by the placement of one object in relationship to another.

Scanner An input device that allows your computer to digitize flat artwork and photographs.

Self-timer A camera function that automatically takes the photograph 10 seconds after the photographer has pushed the shutter-release button.

Sharpness Identifies how "in-focus" a digital image looks.

Shutter The shutter is a curtain located in the camera body that opens and closes in measured increments of time allowing light to reach the film.

Shutter-priority mode An operating mode that allows the photographer to set the shutter speed while the camera selects the aperture opening.

Shutter speed A number that identifies exactly how long or fast the shutter remains open.

Side lighting Side lighting occurs when the light source strikes the subject from the side.

Silhouette A silhouette is an image that shows the solid black shape of an object against a bright background.

Single-use cameras Inexpensive plastic cameras that come with film already loaded and are designed for one-time use.

Slide film Film that reproduces a positive transparency of the image.

SLR (single-lens reflex camera) SLRs are 35mm cameras that have interchangeable lenses.

Soft light Light quality created when the light source is diffused or scattered resulting in a low-contrast scene.

Software Software is a "program" that enables your computer to perform specific functions.

Subject mode An operating mode designed for use with specific subjects such as landscape, portraiture, close-up and action/sports.

Sync speed or synchronization speed The shutter speed that coincides with the light output from the flash.

Telephoto lens A telephoto lens produces a narrow angle of view and compresses the image by making objects in the scene appear closer together. Common telephoto lenses for 35mm cameras are 80mm, 120mm and 200mm.

Top lighting Top lighting occurs from a light source hitting the top of your subject.

Transforming scale Using scale in such a way that changes our understanding of the actual size of objects in the scene.

Transparency Film that reproduces a positive transparent image or slide.

Tripod An adjustable stand with three legs designed to stabilize a camera.

Tungsten-balanced film Film designed to reproduce accurate color in tungsten light conditions.

Underexposure An exposure that is caused by not enough light reaching the film resulting in an image that is very dark with little to no details in the shadow areas.

Visual dynamics The formal qualities of a photograph that give the image visual impact.

Visualize To imagine exactly how the image will or could look in a photograph.

Wide-angle lens For 35mm cameras common wide-angle lenses are 24mm, 28mm and 35mm. A wide-angle lens will reproduce a wider view capturing more of the scene than a normal lens.

Zoom lens A zoom lens incorporates many focal lengths such as 28mm, 50mm and 80mm into one lens. The lens can shift from a wide-angle, through normal to a telephoto view, by simply turning a ring on the lens barrel or pressing a button on the camera body.

About the Author

Joann Zocchi is an assistant professor of photography at the University of Colorado at Denver and Health Sciences Center. For the past 15 years Joann's photographic work has explored the complex relationship between wildlife and human concerns. In 2003 Zocchi was named a Fellow of the John Simon Guggenheim Foundation. Before arriving in Denver, Joann taught photography and digital imaging at The School of Art and Design/Alfred University in Alfred, New York, and Princeton University in New Jersey. She is an active member of the Society for Photographic Education, serving on committees for the national board and organizing regional conferences. Joann was co-founder of Progetto Perugia, a studio art program in Perugia, Italy. She was a member of the Electronic Institute for the Arts at Alfred University and helped to organize the cross-disciplinary conference titled *Text and Image* also at Alfred. She was curator of the Women's Study Gallery at Princeton University and curated a show of contemporary photography at the School of Art and Design, Alfred University. She received her BFA and MFA from the Massachusetts College of Art in Boston, Massachusetts. Selected exhibitions include Princeton University Art Museum; Center for Photography at Woodstock, New York; Southern Light Gallery at Amarillo College, Texas; the Roy H. Parks School of Communication at Ithaca College, New York; Robert C. May Gallery at the University of Kentucky; University of California, Berkeley Extension Center; and Tyler School of Art, Philadelphia. Visiting Artist Talks include State University of New Mexico; Knox College; Hampden Sydney College, Virginia; Colorado State University and Ball State University. Collections include New Mexico State University at Las Cruces, Princeton University Art Museum and the Danforth Museum of Art.

Credits

PAGE 1 THE COLORS OF TAOS

Photos: Joann & Andrea Zocchi; page design: Shannon Taylor, Bristol, Tennessee

Supplies: Texture gel (Liquitex); paint (Making Memories); dimensional glaze (JudiKins); cross (American Traditional Designs); transparency (Magic Scraps); conchos; brads

PAGE 4 CAPTURING CONNOR 101

Photos and page design: Susan Cyrus, Broken Arrow, Oklahoma

Supplies: Cardstocks (Bazzill); ribbon; camera-graphic transparency (Design Originals); transparency; stained-glass paint on letter C (Krylon)

PAGE 4 OUR FIRST VACATION

Photos: Joann & Andrea Zocchi; page design: Holly VanDyne, Mansfield, Ohio

Supplies: Paper (Bazzill); transparency overlay, chipboard letters (Li'l Davis Designs); stamps (PSX Design)

PAGE 4 JUNGLE FEVER

Photos: Joann Zocchi; page design: MaryAnn Wise, The Woodlands, Texas

Supplies: Patterned papers (Creative Imaginations, Wordsworth)

PAGE 5 WORKING AT THE CARWASH

Photos: Joann Zocchi; page design: Cherie Ward, Colorado Springs, Colorado

Supplies: Patterned papers (KI Memories); definition (Making Memories); tag, tab, date rub-ons (Autumn Leaves); sticker letters (C-Thru Ruler, KI Memories, Sticker Studio); ribbon; rickrack; ink

PAGE 5 MY SISTER, MY FRIEND

Photo: Joann Zocchi; page design: Denise Tucker, Versailles, Indiana

Supplies: Patterned paper (Basic Grey); foam paper (Darice); fabric, buttons (Junkitz); acrylic bookplates (DMD); sticker letters, brads, ribbon (Making Memories); decoupage medium (Plaid); metallic rub-ons (Craf-T); grommet (Chatterbox); thread

PAGE 5 OUR SUNNY FROSTY

Photos: Joann Zocchi; page design: Barb Hogan, Cincinnati, Ohio

Supplies: Paper (American Crafts, Bazz- ill); stickers (American Crafts); rub-on letters, buttons (Making Memories); twine (Stampin' Up!)

PAGE 6 FAMILY

Photo: Joann Zocchi; page design: Jodi Amidei, Memory Makers Books

Supplies: Patterned paper (Creative Imaginations, It Takes Two); skeleton leaves (Graphic Products Corp.); brads (Karen Foster Design); dried flowers (Nature's Pressed); dimensional glaze (DecoArt); label holder

PAGE 9 TIKI PARTY

Photos: Joann Zocchi; page design: Jodi Amidei, Memory Makers Books

Supplies: Patterned paper (Basic Grey); textured cardstock (Canson); vellum (Paper Adventures); punch (Nankong); chalk (Craf-T); brads; ink

PAGE 12 FLORENCE, ITALY

Photos: Joann Zocchi; page design: Joanna Bolick, Fletcher, North Carolina

Supplies: Patterned paper, cardstock (Rusty Pickle); rub-ons (American Traditional Designs)

PAGE 18

Photo: Andrea Zocchi © All rights reserved.

PAGE 19 GREAT KIDS

Photos & page design: Paula DeReamer, Alexandria, Minnesota

Supplies: Patterned paper (Chatterbox, Scrapworks); cardstocks (Bazzill, Rusty Pickle); stamps (Close To My Heart, Making Memories); ribbon; copper brads; paint (DecoArt, Making Memories)

PAGE 22 LITTLE LU

Photos: Andrea Zocchi; page design: Shelby Valadez, Saugus, California

Supplies: Patterned paper (7 Gypsies); stamp (Hero Arts); ink; thread

PAGE 29 COLORS

Photos: Joann Zocchi; page design: Jodi Amidei, Memory Makers Books

Supplies: Patterned paper (KI Memories); tiles (Little Black Dress Designs)

PAGE 39 LIVING HISTORY

Photos & page design: MaryJo Regier, Memory Makers Books

Supplies: Patterned paper (Paper Adventures); vellum; brads

PAGE 41 NATURE BOYS

Photos: Joann Zocchi; page design: Shelley Rankin, Fredericton, New Brunswick, Canada

Supplies: Patterned paper (Basic Grey, Mustard Moon); cardstock (Bazzill); sticker letters (Bo-Bunny, Creative Imaginations, Paper Loft); negative strip (Creative Imaginations); synonym index tab (Autumn Leaves); photo turns, oval pebble (Making Memories); ribbon; tag; corner rounder; date stamp

PAGE 43 DEFYING GRAVITY

Photos: Joann Zocchi; page design: Becky Thompson, Fruitland, Idaho

Supplies: Cardstock (Bazzill); metal letters (JoAnn Fabrics); corner rounder punch; brads

PAGE 49 VIGNETTES OF ITALIAN LIFE

Photos: Joann Zocchi; page design: Leah Blanco Williams, Kansas City, Missouri

Supplies: Patterned Paper (Basic Grey); cardstock (Bazzill); letter stickers (Karen Foster Design); ink

PAGE 56 SNOW STUNTS

Photos: Joann Zocchi; page design, Nicole LaCour, Memory Makers magazine

Supplies: Cardstocks (Bazzill); vellum; fibers; metallic embroidery floss

PAGE 58

Photo: Andrea Zocchi © All rights reserved.

PAGE 59 ITALY

Photo: Joann Zocchi; page design: Jodi Amidei, Memory Makers Books

Supplies: Patterned papers (Club Scrap, Hot Off The Press, Me and My Big Ideas); patterned vellum, ephemera cut-outs (Hot Off The Press); clips (EK Success); photo turns (7 Gypsies); brads; ribbon; ink

PAGE 62 PUMPKINS, PUMPKINS EVERYWHERE

Photos: Joann Zocchi; page design: Cori Dahmen, Vancouver, Washington

Supplies: Patterned paper (Carolee's Creations); die-cut letters (QuicKutz); brads (Scrap Arts); paint (Delta); metal tags, stamps (Making Memories); embroidery floss; transparency

PAGE 71 LUCA FISH

Photos: Joann Zocchi; page design: Laurel Gervitz, Maple Grove, Minnesota

Supplies: Patterned papers (Club Scrap, Li'l Davis Designs); transparency

PAGE 78 A MEDIEVAL AFFAIR

Photos: Joann Zocchi; page design: Bay Loftis, Philadelphia, Tennessee

Supplies: Patterned paper, canvas sticker letters (Club Scrap); tile letter (EK Success); rub-on letters (Making Memories); ribbon; watercolor pencils; pens

PAGE 88

Photo: Andrea Zocchi © All rights reserved.

PAGE 89 HAWAIIAN HONEYMOON

Photos: Andrea Zocchi; page design: Pamela James, Ventura, California

Supplies: Patterned paper (source unknown); cardstocks; transparency; chalk (Craf-T); eyelets; bamboo stickers (EK Success); fibers; sticker letters (Creative Imaginations)

PAGE 93 BUILD A BEAR BIRTHDAY

Photos: Joann Zocchi; page design: MaryJo Regier, Memory Makers Books

Supplies: Patterned papers (Karen Foster Design); bear stamp (Kodomo); decorative clips; fibers; slide mount; lettering template (Crafter's Workshop)

PAGE 97 FIELD DAY

Photos: Joann Zocchi; page design: Jennifer Bourgeault, Macomb Township, Michigan

Supplies: Patterned Paper (Daisy D's); letter stickers (Paper Loft, Sticker Studio); circle punch (Creative Memories); stitched circle (Autumn Leaves); "be playful" tag (Me & My Big Ideas); brad; thread

Special Credit:

Epson America, Inc.

The majority of the photographs in this book were scanned on an Epson Perfection 4870 Pro Scanner and production of this book was assisted by an Epson 2200 Printer, Epson papers and Epson inks.

Sources

7 Gypsies
(800) 588-6707
www.7gypsies.com

American Crafts
(800) 879-5185
www.americancrafts.com

American Tombow, Inc.
(800) 835-3232
www.tombowusa.com

American Traditional Designs®
(800) 448-6656
www.americantraditional.com

Apple Computer, Inc.
(800) MY-APPLE
www.apple.com

Autumn Leaves (wholesale only)
(800) 588-6707
www.autumnleaves.com

Basic Grey™
(801) 451-6006
www.basicgrey.com

Bazzill Basics Paper
(480) 558-8557
www.bazzillbasics.com

Bo-Bunny Press
(801) 771-4010
www.bobunny.com

Canon U.S.A., Inc
(516) 328-5000
www.usa.canon.com

Canson, Inc.®
(800) 628-9283
www.canson-us.com

Carolee's Creations®
(435) 563-1100
www.ccpaper.com

Chatterbox, Inc.
(208) 939-9133
www.chatterboxinc.com

Clearsnap, Inc.
(800) 448-4862
www.clearsnap.com

Close To My Heart®
(888) 655-6552
www.closetomyheart.com

Club Scrap™
(888) 634-9100
www.clubscrap.com

Craf-T Products
(507) 235-3996
www.craf-tproducts.com

Crafter's Workshop, The
(877) CRAFTER
www.thecraftersworkshop.com

Creative Imaginations
(wholesale only)
(800) 942-6487
www.cigift.comcom

Creative Memories®
(800) 468-9335
www.creativememories.com

C-Thru® Ruler Company, The
(wholesale only)
(800) 243-8419
www.cthruruler.com

Daisy D's Paper Company
(888) 601-8955
www.daisydspaper.com

Darice, Inc.
(800) 321-1494
www.darice.com

DecoArt™, Inc.
(800) 367-3047
www.decoart.com

Delta Technical Coatings, Inc.
(800) 423-4135
www.deltacrafts.com

Design Originals
(800) 877-7820
www.d-originals.com

DMC Corp.
(973) 589-8931
www.dmc.com

DMD Industries, Inc.
(800) 805-9890
www.dmdind.com

Duracell
www.duracell.com

Eastman Kodak Company
(770) 522-2542
www.kodak.com

EK Success™, Ltd.
(wholesale only)
(800) 524-1349
www.eksuccess.com

Energizer Holdings, Inc.
(800) 383-7323
www.energizer.com

E.P. Levine, Inc.
23 Drydock Avenue
Boston, Massachusetts 02210
(617) 951-1499
www.cameras.com

Epson America, Inc.
(800) GO-EPSON
www.epson.com

Expressions Photography
211 W. County Line Road
Littleton, Colorado 80129
(303) 730-8638
spexpressionsinc@aol.com

Fuji Photo Film U.S.A., Inc.
(800) 755-3854
www.fujifilm.com

Graphic Products Corp.
(800) 323-1660
www.gpcpapers.com

Hero Arts® Rubber Stamps, Inc.
(wholesale only)
(800) 822-4376
www.heroarts.com

Highsmith, Inc.
(800) 554-4661
www.highsmith.com

Hot Off The Press, Inc.
(800) 227-9595
www.paperpizazz.com

It Takes Two®
(800) 331-9843
www.ittakestwo.com

Jo-Ann Fabrics & Crafts
(888) 739-4120
www.joann.com

JudiKins
(310) 515-1115
www.judikins.com

Junkitz™
(212) 944-4250
www.junkitz.com

Karen Foster Design™
(wholesale only)
(801) 451-9779
www.karenfosterdesign.com

KI Memories
(469) 633-9665
www.kimemories.com

Kodomo, Inc.
(650) 589-8681
www.kodomoinc.com

Konica Minolta Photo Imaging
U.S.A., Inc.
(800) 285-6422
www.konicaminolta.com

Krylon®
(216) 566-2000
www.krylon.com

Li'l Davis Designs
(949) 838-0344
www.lildavisdesigns.com

Liquitex® Artist Materials
(888) 4-ACRYLIC
www.liquitex.com

Little Black Dress Designs
(360) 894-8844
www.littleblackdressdesigns.com

Magic Scraps™
(972) 385-1838
www.magicscraps.com

Making Memories
(800) 286-5263
www.makingmemories.com

Marvy® Uchida
(800) 541-5877
www.uchida.com

me & my BiG ideas®
(wholesale only)
(949) 583-2065
www.meandmybigideas.com

Mustard Moon™
(408) 229-8542
www.mustardmoon.com

Nankong Enterprises, Inc.
(302) 731-2995
www.nankong.com

Nature's Pressed
(800) 850-2499
www.naturespressed.com

Olympus® America, Inc.
(800) 645-8160
www.olympusamerica.com

Paper Adventures®
(wholesale only)
(800) 727-0699
www.paperadventures.com

Plaid Enterprises, Inc.
(800) 842-4197
www.plaidonline.com

Polaroid Corp.
(781) 386-2000
www.polaroid.com

Print File®, Inc.
(800) 508-8539
www.printfile.com

PSX Design™
(800) 782-6748
www.psxdesign.com

QuicKutz®
(888) 702-1146
www.quickutz.com

Rusty Pickle
(801) 272-2280
www.rustypickle.com

ScrapArts
(503) 631-4893
www.scraparts.com

Scrapworks™, LLC
(801) 363-1010
www.scrapworks.com

Staedtler®, Inc.
(800) 927-7723
www.staedtler.us

Stampin' Up!®
(800) 782-6787
www.stampinup.com

Sticker Studio™
(208) 322-2465
www.stickerstudio.com

Wordsworth
(719) 282-3495
www.wordsworthstamps.com

X-Acto®, a division of Hunt
Corporation
(800) 283-1707
www.hunt-corp.com

Index